CHRISTIAN ETHICS
A BRIEF HISTORY

W9-BXD-546

BLACKWELL BRIEF HISTORIES OF RELIGION SERIES

This series offers brief, accessible and lively accounts of key topics within theology and religion. Each volume presents both academic and general readers with a selected history of topics which have had a profound effect on religious and cultural life. The word 'history' is, therefore, understood in its broadest cultural and social sense. The volumes are based on serious scholarship but they are written engagingly and in terms readily understood by general readers.

Published

Heaven	Alister E. McGrath
Heresy	G. R. Evans
Islam	Tamara Sonn
Death	Douglas J. Davies
Saints	Lawrence S. Cunningham
Christianity	Carter Lindberg
Dante	Peter S. Hawkins
Spirituality	Philip Sheldrake
Cults and New Religions	Douglas E. Cowan and David G. Bromley
Love	Carter Lindberg
Christian Mission	Dana L. Robert
Christian Ethics	Michael Banner

Forthcoming

Judaism	Steven Leonard Jacobs
Reformation	Kenneth Appold
Monasticism	Dennis D. Martin
Apocalypse	Martha Himmelfarb
Shinto	John Breen and Mark Teeuwen
Sufism	Shahzad Green

CHRISTIAN ETHICS
A BRIEF HISTORY

Michael Banner

WILEY-BLACKWELL

A John Wiley & Sons, Ltd., Publication

This edition first published 2009
© 2009 Michael Banner

Blackwell Publishing was acquired by John Wiley & Sons in February 2007. Blackwell's publishing program has been merged with Wiley's global Scientific, Technical, and Medical business to form Wiley-Blackwell.

Registered Office
John Wiley & Sons Ltd, The Atrium, Southern Gate, Chichester, West Sussex, PO19 8SQ, United Kingdom

Editorial Offices
350 Main Street, Malden, MA 02148-5020, USA
9600 Garsington Road, Oxford, OX4 2DQ, UK
The Atrium, Southern Gate, Chichester, West Sussex, PO19 8SQ, UK

For details of our global editorial offices, for customer services, and for information about how to apply for permission to reuse the copyright material in this book please see our website at www.wiley.com/wiley-blackwell.

The right of Michael Banner to be identified as the author of this work has been asserted in accordance with the Copyright, Designs and Patents Act 1988.

All rights reserved. No part of this publication may be reproduced, stored in a retrieval system, or transmitted, in any form or by any means, electronic, mechanical, photocopying, recording or otherwise, except as permitted by the UK Copyright, Designs and Patents Act 1988, without the prior permission of the publisher.

Wiley also publishes its books in a variety of electronic formats. Some content that appears in print may not be available in electronic books.

Designations used by companies to distinguish their products are often claimed as trademarks. All brand names and product names used in this book are trade names, service marks, trademarks or registered trademarks of their respective owners. The publisher is not associated with any product or vendor mentioned in this book. This publication is designed to provide accurate and authoritative information in regard to the subject matter covered. It is sold on the understanding that the publisher is not engaged in rendering professional services. If professional advice or other expert assistance is required, the services of a competent professional should be sought.

A catalogue record for this book is available from the Library of Congress

A catalogue record for this book is available from the British Library.

978-1-4051-1517-9 (hard back)
978-1-4051-1518-6 (paper back)

Set in 12/13pt Sabon
by SPi Publisher Services, Pondicherry, India
Printed in Singapore

1   2009

To Francis Woolley and to the parishes and people of West Wratting and Weston Colville, in gratitude for their skills in the practice of ethics

Contents

Preface

It is something of a truism that short books take longer to write than long books, and this book has been more years in the making than a long book might have been. It was twice delayed by moves – in the first place from London to Edinburgh, and then from Edinburgh to Cambridge. It has been completed in Cambridge, within the walls of Trinity College, in conditions so favorable to academic endeavor that had I not finished it, I would have been quite without excuse.

The book was begun whilst I was working at King's College, in the University of London, and living in West Wratting, close by Weston Colville, not far from Newmarket, and it is to the parishes, people, and vicar of those two villages that this book is dedicated, with warmest thanks for their gracious friendship and hospitality during the three years I was resident. After I had left, Brian and Ruth Hazelman generously let me retreat from time to time, to the converted barn at the end of their garden to try to finish this book; their kindness was mixed with such dismay at my lack of progress that I was spurred to do better. George and Jane Cassidy have proved true and constant friends over very many years and I owe them immense gratitude. I rather think that all of the above have nothing much to learn from a work on ethics.

As the book was nearing completion a current colleague, Dr Jeremy Butterfield, a Senior Research of Trinity, was kind enough to read the manuscript closely and offer (gentle) criticism and (generous) encouragement. (This was all the more generous since it is inconceivable that I shall be able to return the favor by reading drafts of his papers in the more abstruse regions of the philosophy of physics.) A former colleague, Mr. Eric Southworth, Senior Tutor of St. Peter's College, Oxford, has, since I was a Research Fellow at St. Peter's, been unflagging in offering support and wisdom, and was true to form in reviewing the penultimate draft. His judgment is one I value very highly indeed.

Sally-Ann Gannon has seen the book through from beginning to end and is a star and a dote. She will probably be even more delighted than I am to see it dispatched to the press.

MB
Trinity College
Cambridge
July 2008

Introduction

The aim of this book, as the title indicates, is to provide a brief history of Christian ethics. Why might this be a worthwhile task and what are the problems with accomplishing it?

Ethics itself needs no apology it seems. It is a subject of abiding interest – at least as a matter for discussion and debate, if not for practice. The latest development in our knowledge of genetics announced by some laboratory; a case in a hospital which seems to pose a particular dilemma; or the threat of armed intervention by a foreign power in another nation's internal disputes – all these and more find the newspapers, television, and radio offering reflections on the rights and wrongs of the matter in hand.

Nor does the word "brief" need an apology either, since the ethics which is found in everyday life is very often brief. As Engels once said: "It is the height of open-mindedness in an Englishman to think that there are two sides to every question" – and, as he might have added, to think that these two sides can be fully aired, and an appropriate adjudication between them made, in an article filling that very particular and well-defined space assigned for just such pieces on the editorial pages of what is referred to as the "quality press."

"Brief Ethics," then, are all to the good it seems, but what about the addition of the words "History" and "Christian"? Ethics may be in demand, and especially abbreviated versions, but what of histories of ethics, or even histories of Christian ethics? Let's take "History" first.

The aforementioned "Brief Ethics" of contemporary punditry is little inclined to be interested in history. The principles and contentions of popular debate are likely to be presented as immediately compelling, with little or no indication of an interest in (or sense of) their origins or source. Nor, if one moves up from the level of newspaper commentary to the slightly larger canvas of books, does the situation seem to alter dramatically. It is not uncommon to read entire volumes, especially in the area of what is termed "bioethics," which have but the scarcest references to any figure from the past, and really seem to think that ethics is a bold new venture which "began near the midpoint of the twentieth century."[1] Many proceed, in other words, as if we are the very first people to think about the moral questions which confront us; or at least, even if we are not the very first, that those who went before have nothing to teach us.

Of course these notions – that we are the first people to think about these questions, or that those who went before have nothing to teach us – are not the same, and they may have different roots. The thought that we are the first people to think about ethical questions is, of course, straightforwardly false, though it is true that the ancient Greeks were insouciant in relation to such matters as cloning or global warming. So if we think that the really interesting and difficult questions are the ones which are in this sense contemporary, then we may think of ourselves as, to all intents and purposes, in uncharted waters.

This reason for neglecting what may have been thought before is, however, shallow. Nuclear weapons are new, but not the question as to whether it is ethical to aim at the deaths of non-combatants in the prosecution of war. Cloning may be new too, but not the question as to what is required by a respect for the dignity of the individual. Climate change may be a new challenge, but probably not the question as to what are the proper limits of our making and shaping of nature. The very particular issues which trouble us may in some sense be new, and these new issues may challenge our ethical thinking and action in new ways. They may lead us to new insights and even

[1]   R. E. Bulger, E. Heitman, and S. J. Reiser, eds., *The Ethical Dimensions of the Biological Sciences* (Cambridge, 1993), 1.

to reject certain accepted truths and principles – but the questions which these new eventualities pose in very particular ways are not themselves wholly unprecedented, and it would be implausible to think that what we have to do is to invent a subject from scratch.

The assumption that the past has nothing to say on the subject which concerns us is false, and therefore cannot justify our putting history to one side. But can we ignore it on the ground that the past has nothing to say worth our hearing? Such an arrogant thought is not often expressed explicitly, but implicitly it seems to hold a certain sway. It finds its neatest implicit endorsement in the conviction of many an examination essay that the chief and insurmountable difficulty in the thought of, say, Thomas Aquinas, lies in its being medieval. (Indeed, so compelling is this objection thought to be, that the prosecution does not trouble to offer further evidence against the accused, who is, after all, hardly in a position to deny the charge.) But if the undergraduate essay reveals its underlying thought with the bold confidence of youth, the same attitude is revealed, albeit with none of this youthful candor, in countless other ways. Witness the already mentioned paucity of historical reference and engagement in so many articles and books on ethics, including ones which sometimes slip the word "Christian" into the title. There is very often nothing to indicate the slightest expectation that history has anything to say worth our hearing and worth adding to our brief ethics.

Two rather different thoughts can be offered in the first instance, not aimed at justifying the interest in history as such, since that justification must finally be *a posteriori*, not *a priori* – warranted, that is to say, by what follows, not by what can be said at the outset – but aimed, rather, at sufficiently weakening the prejudice against history to encourage those who might be otherwise disinclined to venture a little further.

The first thought is *ad hominem*. The spirit of the age is one which, in its official pronouncements at least, is accepting of cultural pluralism, in the sense that we are generally averse to saying of one culture that it is better than another; we are more comfortable with the thought that cultures are different. But then the question arises: how is it that we are unwilling to judge cultures which are contemporaneous with our own, but only too willing to dismiss ones which are not? Of course, we might suppose that the culture of the medieval West can be dismissed just because it is a predecessor culture to our own, whereas Buddhist culture, in its twenty-first-century instantiations, is plainly not. Analogously, I may be unwilling to assert that a Mercedes is better than a tractor, but perfectly happy to assert that the Mercedes mark 1 has been superseded by the mark 2 or the mark 3. This line of thought is, however, problematic. It only escapes the *ad hominem* charge of inconsistency by claiming that the road from the past to the present is of such a kind that we can confidently dismiss what preceded us whilst remaining open-minded to all that did not. It at once presupposes an extraordinarily confident and optimistic account of the way in which a culture betters itself, whilst holding to an extra-ordinarily diffident and agnostic account of our ability to judge all others but these predecessors. Tightropes can indeed be walked, but when there are alternative routes, and one is not simply out for thrills, it may be worth considering them.

There is another argument for treating history with some respect and as a matter of interest, and this argument is not simply *ad hominem*. Alastair MacIntyre is not alone among contemporary critics of modernity in thinking that the modern West is, morally speaking, in a state. In his influential book *After Virtue*, he suggested that, as a culture and individually, we are morally confused and in disarray, unable to resolve differences amongst ourselves and even, so to speak, with our-selves.[2] Neither as a society, nor typically as individuals, are we possessed of a coherent moral framework within which our actions, attitudes, and evaluations make sense. And part of the explanation for this, so he and others have wanted to say, is that we are inheritors of different and competing moral traditions which have come down to us in bits and pieces and which do not, so to speak, add up. MacIntyre's example of

---

[2]   London, 1981.

contemporary disagreement seemingly incapable of rational solution is that surrounding abortion. Here, two or more traditions of thought meet and contest but with no obvious basis for resolving the conflict. On the one side there are those who contend for the sanctity of life, on the other those who press for the right to choose. But these two sides have no obvious recourse to thoughts and principles which would reconcile this conflict; which is why, says MacIntyre, the debate about abortion seems like no debate at all. Our plight, MacIntyre alleges, is the plight of those dwelling among the ruins of diverse moral traditions.

Even granted the premise of confusion, further argument and evidence would be needed if one were to establish the truth of that supposed explanation. However that might be, even as a hypothesis the diagnosis is surely sufficient encouragement to wonder where our less than wholly systematized moral beliefs and attitudes have come from, and furthermore whether we might gain some understanding and insight by delving into their source and origins. Whether or not we fully accept MacIntyre's account, it seems unlikely that we have nothing to gain from the attempt to try to understand how we have come to the views we have.

If so, then we have found a reason for rejecting "A Brief Ethics" in favor of "A Brief History of Ethics." But what, finally, of the qualifier "Christian" placed before "Ethics"? How is that to be commended to the attention and interest of those who are perhaps willing to take on the need for history, but are doubtful of the point or value of this further qualification? Sure enough they may be persuaded of the prima facie merit of gaining a historical perspective, but why should that historical perspective be provided from the vantage point of Christianity?

The blunt and pragmatic answer is just that the story of ethics in the West has been, at its core, the story of Christian ethics. This is not, let it be noted, a claim about the present authority of Christianity or about its hold on contemporary intellectual and moral allegiances, but rather about the part it has had in shaping the practices, attitudes, and values of everyday life. A contemporary writer elegantly pointed to this truth in an aside alleging that "the idea of human dignity" is "the moral effluvium of a discredited metaphysics"[3] (the "discredited metaphysics" being Christianity, of course). Now if this is arguably true of the notion of human dignity, it is also possibly true of other of our everyday values and attitudes, no matter our rejections or repudiations or simple ignorance of Christianity; these may have their source (and quite possibly their sense), in this "discredited metaphysics." Our attitudes to birth and death, love and sex, nature and art, work and wealth, authority and freedom, law and justice, certainly emerged in a world in which this "metaphysics," whether now "discredited" or not, provided the framework for thought and action. Thus if history has a place in giving us an understanding of the moral concepts, categories, and expectations which shape our world (where "our" means "the modern West's"), that history has to be in large part the history of Christian life and thought.

This is neither to deny nor to overlook a whole list of truths which might seem to count against the contention that a history of the ethics of the West is primarily a history of Christian ethics. There is the fact, for example, that Christian ethics drew upon existing Greek and Jewish ideas, so much so that some have wanted to speak of these, along with other philosophies and codes, as providing "sources" of Christian ethics. There is also the undoubted truth that besides any matter of sources, Christian ethics has not held the field alone but, throughout its history, came into contact with, and has been influenced by, other systems of thought and ways of life: in the Middle Ages the contact was with Judaism and Islam, and in the modern period with a whole host of other traditions, religious and non-religious. And then there is the point – one which a contemporary objector might stress most keenly – that there has always been vigorous and vocal dissent directed against Christianity, particularly in the modern period. How can one claim that the history of ethics in the West is centrally the story of Christian ethics when that history plainly includes, to limit ourselves to

---

[3]   J. Rachels, *Created from Animals* (London, 1990), 5.

the relatively recent past, such prominent and vociferous doubters as Bentham, Marx, and Nietzsche, amongst others?

Sure enough there have been a variety of influences, other and competing traditions, and prominent voices raised in protest at or rejection of Christianity. But in the history of the West, they have been just that from the perspective of what has been central: that is, various and other influences and traditions. Even the most eloquent and passionate opponents of Christianity, such as Nietzsche, suffer the pathos of finding themselves located in the history of Christian ethics for the very reason that their dissent is dissent *from* Christianity. They are in that sense "reactionary" and a part of a story even as they seek to bring that story to a close and begin a new one.

The claim that the history of ethics in the West is, in a sense, the history of Christian ethics can very well admit and acknowledge that Christianity has itself been influenced, as well as opposed, by other traditions and ways of thought. It can allow just as well that our moral and social world could so change that a history of Christian thought would cease to provide a helpful perspective on the past. But whilst allowing all this, it might still insist that in telling a story which promises to make sense of where we are now, the birth and growth of Christianity must provide a dominant motif.

For all that this answer is, as I believe, true, it fails to stir the blood. To say that we should embark upon a study of Christian ethics because Christian ethics has been very influential in shaping our understandings of ourselves, society, and the world is all very well, but it sounds slightly worthy. It seems a bit like recommending the study of Latin because the Romans were very important and have influenced how we are in countless ways. As it stands, this justification for the study of the history of Christian ethics sounds as though we might simply note the influence of the past and move on – just as we might learn with surprise and wonder how very significant the Romans were in determining the present, without feeling in the least moved to embrace the Latin language.

The quotation from Rachels indicates, however, that matters don't stand quite like that in relation to this history. The Romans may, in part, have made us the people we are today, but we can very well continue to be those people, with or without any acknowledgment of them. Not so, at least arguably, with Christianity. If Rachels is right that such a cherished idea as, for example, the idea of human dignity may be declared "effluvium" if Christian metaphysics belongs only in history books, then the question of the continuing value of Christian ethics can hardly be a matter of mere academic interest (using "academic" in its usual pejorative sense). It may be that other of our values, equally central to who we are and how we live, have roots in Christianity. If so, the validity of this history, so to speak, is a more than worthy question. Rather it is a question about whether and how we can frame our individual and social lives, and what sort of world there will be, if these values are deemed to have lost their power just because of their dependence on outmoded beliefs. This book doesn't set out to answer the question of the truth of Christianity as such. Its task is to expound the ethical implications of Christian belief, not to consider the grounds for that belief, nor to commend it. But as it seeks to explore those implications, it may pose the more sharply the question whether this history can serve to govern our future.

Our first question was whether the task of offering a brief history of Christian ethics deserves our attention and we have argued that it does. Having noted that the task is worthwhile, we need also to note that it is not without its difficulties.

To notice one such difficulty serves as a very important reminder of what ethics is really about, certainly as the Christian tradition has considered it. Ethics is, of course, concerned with what one should do and therefore its essential expression is in action. Now amongst all the things which Christians have done by way of expressing their convictions in deeds, writing books with titles such as "An Outline of Christian Ethics" or "A Guide to Christian Ethics" has played a very minor part. Far more important than that has been founding and running hospitals, establishing schools, campaigning for changes in the law, entering monasteries, pleading for clemency for condemned prisoners, going on crusade, or perhaps refusing to fight in a war. Even if we exclude such things from consideration and allow ourselves only to weigh like against like, we would have to note that books of explicit ethical instruction and argument are, both in volume and probably significance, less weighty than books of sermons, hymns, prayers, and poems. Not least (and it is very much indeed), these other sources might keep us grounded in what is taken for granted and beyond dispute, and therefore left unsaid in other books which are very often rather explicitly the products of controversy and contention.

Thus, if we were to seek to understand the moral landscape which Christians have construed, constructed, and inhabited, the sources on which we would need to draw would be various and vast. A brief history, as this one is, finds itself embarrassed in dealing even half-adequately with explicitly intellectual history – that is, with the major texts in the tradition of writing about Christian ethics and how it is to be conceived – let alone in throwing the net more widely still. History of any kind, long or short, involves making choices or discriminations, to use a term which immediately indicates what is at stake, and in a brief history these choices are the more constrained, and the discriminations the more acute. The story we shall unfold will have to be told with a broad sweep, taking in only the major features of the landscape, but leaving much of the terrain unremarked and unnoticed. Such a story may enable readers to get their bearings and to explore for themselves; but it cannot hope to be a substitute for that exploration.

There is a little text from early in the Christian tradition which provides a very good starting point for our journey. In due course, we shall have to go behind, not just beyond, it in telling our story. But as it stands, it opens to us, if we will attend to it, the interiority of the Christian life. It is neither an academic disquisition, nor a contribution to debate; it is a call to live thus and so. And this, we shall do well to remember, is what Christian ethics has been about.

1

Benedict and the Practice of the Christian Life

Around 1,500 years ago (circa 550), somewhere (probably in Italy), someone (we can't be sure who) wrote a very short work (no more than about forty pages in a standard modern paperback), which provides us with what can plausibly be seen as Christianity's paradigmatic framing and answering of the question of ethics.

To modern eyes, however, the *Rule of St Benedict* is a very curious document indeed, and its relevance to our subject not immediately obvious. Within its brief span it is concerned with a great variety of seemingly arcane questions: "at what seasons alleluia is to be said" is the issue settled in chapter 15; chapter 55 has as its theme "the clothes and shoes of the brethren"; "the appointment of the abbot" is addressed in chapter 64. Indeed, in the totality of its themes and subjects it bears little resemblance to any contemporary genre of literature with which we are likely to be familiar, and it certainly doesn't look much like a contribution to the subject of ethics as it is commonly construed. For ethics has come to be thought of as a subject which has to do especially with thinking about hard cases, so that mention of it is likely to bring to mind a set of vexed contemporary problems, probably including issues such as abortion, euthanasia, and the rights and wrongs of declaring and conducting war. On these matters the *Rule of St Benedict* is silent. Add to this the fact that the *Rule* is a rule for monks, and the relevance of this text to our subject seems far from obvious.

It would be a mistake, however, to allow a simple unfamiliarity to prevent our considering the possibility that what we have before us in the *Rule* is not outside our subject, but rather an important contribution to that subject conceived in a way which is currently unfashionable. The *Rule of St Benedict* is not about what to do in hard cases, but it is plainly about what to do. It is, in fact, a rule for life, keeping company with the classical tradition in addressing and answering the broad question, "What is it to live well?" That is say, then, that it finds the ethical question to be general and fundamental, and not simply one which crops up in particularly trying and difficult circumstances. It is a question which is, on the contrary, basic and all-encompassing. Moreover, and to address the second concern about the *Rule*'s relevance, the *Rule*, as we shall see, although addressed specifically to monks, provides an account of what it is to live well which is more widely relevant. It may contain certain specifics and particularities relating to the monastic life, but in its central concerns it is, in effect, addressed to all.

The *Rule*, however, is concerned not only with a "what," but also with a "how" and a "why," and these further concerns may add to a contemporary sense of its oddity. It certainly has an account of *what* it is to live a properly human life, to which we shall turn in a moment. But in addition it addresses the question, which is by no means deemed compulsory for ethics in general, of *how* it is possible for us to live thus and so. That is, it does not simply posit, as it might, an account of what it is to live well, but is concerned with how we may achieve that at which we should aim in life. And furthermore, albeit implicitly, it provides an answer to another question: *why*, we might ask Benedict (conventionally deemed the author), "Why do you say what you say – that is, with what authority do you propose the content of, and the method for, the good life?"

What is it to live well? How can we do so? And why should we do so? To these three questions the *Rule* contains an answer, and one which, in its broad shape and substance, is a model answer for the mainline Christian tradition.

The *Rule*'s most general answer to the "What?" question is in the chapter "The Tools of Good Works" and is borrowed from the Bible: "to love the Lord God with all one's heart, all one's soul, and all one's strength. Then, one's neighbour as oneself."[1] Thus to live well is to live in relationship, in a society with two dimensions: a vertical dimension which directs us towards God, and a horizontal dimension which directs us towards our neighbor. But not just to live in any sort of relationship to them, since we can be in relationship to others when we compete with them, or are hostile towards them, or simply use them for our own advantage as need arises. Rather we are to be ordered to God and neighbor in a relationship characterized by love.

Suppose for the moment that we remove God from the picture. It would then, perhaps, be quite easy to pass by this thought, so familiar is it, without noting something of its particularity. That the good life consists in living in loving community may seem unremarkable. When Aristotle asserted, famously, that man is a political animal, he was asserting what much of the subsequent classical tradition would take for granted, namely that a properly human life is one lived with and alongside others in a polis (city). The use of the evaluative "civilized," containing as it does a reference to the civitas or city, signals a wide acceptance of Aristotle's claim. But it is worth noting that even if Benedict's preference for social life, the life of a "city," is far from unique, it had a certain particularity in his own day and has not been universally accepted subsequently.

In Benedict's day there were other monks, following patterns of life other than the one he commends. Now though in the very first chapter of the *Rule*, Benedict speaks scornfully of some of these ("their law is their own good pleasure"), he mentions with great honor others, the "Anchorites or Hermits," who engage in "the solitary combat of the desert." But although he mentions them with honor, in practice Benedict treats the tradition – which had had as its great heroes Anthony of Egypt and Simon Stylites, famed for their spiritually daring "solitary combat," the latter spending many years atop a pillar in the desert – as an exception and not as a norm. As commentators

---

[1]   *The Rule of St Benedict*, trans. J. McCann (London, 1976), ch. 4; references throughout are to chapter number.

have noted, the outward and visible sign of this turn away from spiritual isolation is in Benedict's preference for the dormitory over the cell. And this is a token of what Benedict is about: devising a rule for life together, in which life, not the solitary life, the individual finds his or her good – so much so, that the dormitory takes the place of the single study bedroom of the earlier tradition.

If Benedict's choice of social life as constitutive of the human good represented a particular decision in his day against competing conceptions of monasticism, it has had a certain particularity subsequently against other conceptions of the good life. Certainly in practice, and sometimes in theory too, there have been numerous conceptions of what it is to live the good life which have either failed, or found it difficult, or denied the need, to conceive of the good of that life as essentially a life with others. That is not to say, of course, that these conceptions have, so to speak, imagined or willed away other beings – although solipsism, either theoretical or practical, is far from unprecedented; Nietzsche, for example, with a certain determination, and likewise with a certain romantic and epic grandeur, sought to dwell in "azure isolation" on his real and metaphoric mountain tops, and so to conceive human life as, in its essence, life alone. But even for those who have not followed that particular path, and have reckoned with a need for the other in conceptualizing the good of life, it has not always been clear what place or role this other has, and thus whether (as Benedict supposes), the very good of life consists in this encounter. There may be various roles, uses, and places for the other, but it may not be as objects of love, with whom and through whom we find a common and shared good. Bentham, with none of the romance and epic of Nietzsche, insisted that there is no such thing as the common good; on the contrary, he contended that the good of society is just the sum of the good of individuals. Thomas Paine had made the same claim. Less romantic and epic than Nietzsche they may be, but Bentham's creed has had far more followers than Nietzsche's ever had – so much so, that in our day it can seem that the very notion of the common good is a matter chiefly of incomprehension or suspicion, or both.

According to Benedict however, our good lies in a life lived in relationship with God and neighbor and, moreover, in a relationship of love. But what is it to love someone? The word "love" is so bandied about that we may forget that it has a cognitive element – that is, it is not a matter of feeling alone, but of feelings and beliefs. To love something requires that we have a belief about the sort of thing it is, and more specifically what its good consists in. Were I to give you a box with the instruction to love its contents you wouldn't know how to go on without taking a look: a pot plant, a Ming vase, a rabbit, would, after all, each require something different.

Benedict is not vague on this subject, but specific. The love which is to be offered to God and neighbor is characterized as service in both cases, but the service of each is, naturally enough, rather different. The service we owe to God is praise, and the *Rule* enjoins a round of worship so full as to astonish all but the most avidly devout. Benedict cites the words of the Psalmist – "Seven times a day have I given praise to thee" – and decrees that "we shall observe this sacred number of seven, if we fulfil the duties of our service in the Hours of Lauds, Prime, Terce, Sext, None, Vespers and Compline."[2] But the same Psalmist also reports, "At midnight I rose to give praise to thee." So, in addition, "let us rise in the night to praise him."[3]

This service of God, as we shall presently see, is thought to be that which enables the service of neighbor, but for the moment we should put that to one side and simply note what that latter service consists in. The service we owe our neighbor is found in a care and regard for the good of the community and for the individuals within and without it. But this care and regard, we should further note, is in various ways subversive of practices, expectations, and patterns of behavior likely as common then as now. The good of the community requires, thinks Benedict, a repudiation of private property ("a most wicked vice"[4]), and

---

[2]   *Rule*, 16, referring to Psalm 128.
[3]   Ibid.
[4]   *Rule*, 33.

likewise of certain patterns of precedence, hierarchy, and governance.

Whilst the repudiation of private property is perhaps the most striking of these points, the conception of good order within the community is just as significant. Notice first that the community is to have its say in the appointment of the abbot.[5] More importantly, in directing the life of the community, the abbot is charged to listen to the advice of all – "as often as any important business has to be done in the monastery, let the abbot call together the whole community."[6] And in council, and elsewhere, he is instructed "not [to] make any distinction of persons."[7] Furthermore, and especially, "let him keep this present Rule"; i.e. himself.[8] In our day we are familiar with various ideas and ideals which these practices might be said to anticipate, such as the need for consent and consultation in ordering a community, and the rule of law, binding even on those who are responsible for its interpretation and application. But here in the *Rule* we find very early expression of such conceptions, which, in virtue of the *Rule*'s huge significance in the shaping of Europe in the so-called Dark Ages, would themselves have great influence in creating prevalent notions of what belongs to the well-being of communities.

Now if the *Rule*'s conception of the proper exercise of authority and power within and by the community represents a challenge to patterns of order, precedence, and hierarchy, which can seem quite natural and certainly are common, so too it represents a challenge to the individual. The monk is required to repudiate those informal, unspoken, patterns of precedence and hierarchy which commonly order not the social but the individual life, and which place his wants and needs before and above all others. Rather, the need of others is to take precedence, and within the monastery special care is to be taken of the young,

---

[5] *Rule*, 64.
[6] *Rule*, 3.
[7] *Rule*, 2.
[8] *Rule*, 64.

the aged, and the sick.[9] In the same way, "In the reception of poor men and pilgrims special attention should be shown, because in them is Christ more truly welcomed; for the fear which the rich inspire is enough of itself to secure them honour."[10]

If the *Rule* advances radical conceptions of what constitutes proper order within social and individual life, notice that it does this for the sake of the good of the community and those whom the community serves. And this good, quite clearly, recognizes that human needs are material – not *only* material, but material nonetheless. Time and again the *Rule* is concerned with "stuff," particularly with food. A monk's life "ought at all times to be lenten,"[11] says Benedict; but the monk's relationship to the world is not one of simple renunciation. The poor are to be clothed and the sick cared for and the hungry fed – these needs are to be met, not denied or overcome, even in the case of monks.

The community which results might be described somewhat awkwardly as a worldly otherworldly community – or, just as well (or just as awkwardly) as an otherworldly worldly community. The monk is not directed to sit in solitary, rigorous, and ascetic contemplation of another realm. Nor is the monk directed to the neighbor and his or her needs just insofar as the neighbor may be assisted in overcoming them and turning away from the world. Rather, while placing all activity in the framework provided by the daily service of God, the monk is to serve the neighbor in the material life of the community, which meets its needs and the needs of others through work and labor. The *Rule* is otherworldly, of course, in conceiving the final or true good of human life by reference to a good which lies outside the world, namely God; and the ordering of human life by reference to this end touches it here and now. But in a way which might have been and was indeed contested, both from within and from outside the Christian tradition, the *Rule* gives an extremely grounded, worldly account of the good life here and now.

[9] *Rule*, 31, 36, and 37.
[10] *Rule*, 53.
[11] *Rule*, 49.

What is it to live well? This is the core question which the *Rule* addresses, and we have seen that the answer is that to live well is to live in community with God and neighbor, finding our good in offering them our loving service: to the one worship, and to the other, aid and fellowship in the very stuff of life.

But if the first question is "*What* is it to live well?" we also noted that Benedict addresses the question of *how* we are to do that – and that might seem to contemporary eyes to be a distinctly optional question for ethics to address. It is enough for many codes of ethics to tell us what to do. But as well as telling us what the good life consists in, the *Rule* is concerned to guide us in how we might achieve this end.

The sense in which this "how" has been considered an optional question becomes clear if we reflect on the fact that when Benedict proposes that his monastery should be "a school of the Lord's service,"[12] this is a school with a quite distinct syllabus. It is concerned above all that we should learn not so much moral knowledge, but, far more importantly, moral obedience. Moral knowledge is far from being the first problem; Benedict has, after all, already told us what the good life consists in, and he indicates no lively sense that acquiring moral knowledge is a matter of great difficulty.

Contrast this with Plato's *Republic* – to mention a great book of the classical world from which Christianity distinguishes itself. In that book, the problem of knowledge seems to dominate, and the difficulty of the acquisition of moral knowledge is expressed in the powerful story of sun and cave. We are like those who dwell in a cave, who see only the flickering shadows cast by a fire, and mistake them for reality. These shadows are but appearances, and reality lies outside the cave and in the bright realm lit by the sun, where we will be first of all blinded by the dazzling light. The task of gaining moral knowledge resembles the task of these cave-dwellers in learning to look at the sun.[13]

---

12   *Rule*, Prologue.
13   Plato, *The Republic*, Book 6; in many translations.

Contemporary thought sometimes seems to doubt the very existence of moral knowledge, although is generally insistent that the existence of certain rights is indubitable. However that may be, it is commonly supposed that finding moral answers to certain questions is very difficult indeed, and that it is the problem of "hard cases" which is *the* problem for ethics. This is not Benedict's view. For Benedict the chief problem is not the problem of knowing what to do, but actually of doing it – it is a problem not of knowledge, but of will. So Benedict does not simply posit a rule for life and then leave it at that, for according to everything he says, the way of life to which we are summoned is not easily and simply within our grasp. It is a "labour" and a "fight" and it requires "strictness of discipline" (all that in the Prologue). The monastery is to be a "school of the Lord's service" and a reading of the *Rule* gives every indication that our study in the way of obedience will be lifelong, for the very reason that we are seeking not to gain knowledge, but to school our ever-ready-to-be-unruly wills.

The Prologue is addressed "to … whosoever thou mayest be that renouncing thine own will to fight for the true King, Christ, dost take up the strong and glorious weapons of obedience." We need to learn obedience, and Benedict thinks in turn that we will only learn that if we gain a very unclassical virtue – Hume would rightfully identify it as "monkish."[14] Benedict treats of it in the longest chapter in the *Rule*, chapter 7: "Of Humility."

That chapter exhaustively, and somewhat exhaustingly, categorizes the steps and stages on the road to humility; indeed, there being 12 such steps seems a pious rather than an analytic necessity. The details are not important; what is important is just that humility has the centrality it does. And it has this centrality just because it is humility which is the basis for our obedience, against which our pride rebels.

This contention only pushes one of Benedict's questions further back. If we need to learn obedience if we are to live the good life in community with God and neighbor, and if we need

14   D. Hume, *An Enquiry Concerning the Principles of Morals*, section 9, in *Enquiries*, ed. L. A. Selby-Bigge, 3rd edn. (Oxford, 1975).

humility if we are to practice obedience, how are we to learn
humility? There are, in turn, two answers to this. First of all,
worship, which determines and marks out the monastic day, is
the practice which expresses and thus teaches the truths which
humility presupposes: that we stand under God as our creator,
and alongside each other as his creatures. As the monk partici-
pates in worship he learns humility just as he listens to the word
of God in the Scriptures, and learns from that to ascribe honor
to God and to God's creation. But the second answer is the
more fundamental: to learn humility we need grace. Benedict's
general injunction applies here: "let us ask God that he be
pleased, where our nature is powerless, to give us the help of
his grace."[15] Our natures fail us, and our wills, in particular, are
feeble things or quite powerless. Knowing what we should do
is not enough; we need also to learn to do it, and this involves
a reordering of the will. Even attendance in the school of obedience, however, is not enough; in addition we stand in need of
assistance from outside ourselves.

We have outlined Benedict's answer to the question *what* it is
to live well, and we have seen that he addresses the question
which many ethical systems seem to treat as optional, namely
the question as to *how* we are to do what we should do. But in
addition to the *what* and the *how*, there remains the *why*. Why
is this account of what the good life is, and the characterization
of what may stand between us and achieving it, to be regarded
as authoritative?

Well, although it will come as no surprise, we should complete
our account of the elements of this paradigmatic conception of
the ethical life, by underlining what may have been obvious,
namely that Benedict does not assert all this on his own authority.
Nor does he assert it as eminently sensible or reasonable.
Explicitly and implicitly, Benedict's authority is the Bible. Of
course, the summation of the tools of good works – "To love
the Lord God with all one's heart, with all one's soul, and all
one's strength. Then, one's neighbour as oneself" – is a quotation

---

[15]   *Rule*, Prologue.

of Jesus's own words from the Gospels. And the further elaboration of these tools makes reference to other such words in the Gospels, as well as in the Epistles and the Old Testament. As any annotated edition will reveal, the text of the *Rule* is saturated with biblical quotations, just as the monks' lives are to be saturated with the Bible: they are to read and hear it day by day, especially the Psalms, and with special solemnity the Gospel, and also the *Rule* itself with all its biblical references. Whatever influences there may be on Benedict's *Rule*, and there are many, the Bible is his chief and ruling authority.

This answer to the question of authority may be misunderstood, however. For there is a way of using the Bible in our day which is not the use which Benedict makes of it, nor the use of those amongst his predecessors from whom he has learnt. For the *Rule* is not, so to say, deduced from the Bible and its instructions are not "proofed" by texts. It is better to say that the *Rule* tries to conceive what it might be to live human life in the light of the story of salvation as the Bible witnesses to it. And this is not a matter of shuffling and rearranging a few key quotations. It is, in fact, a matter of wide-ranging theological reflection and thought, grounded in the Bible to be sure, but not in any simple way read off from it. (It is for this very reason that this book has avoided the temptation of beginning with a chapter on the Bible, since such a chapter might very well encourage misconceptions involved in many "uses" of the Bible. Another way to make the underlying point would be to say that *A Brief History of Physics* would not begin with a chapter on reality; not because reality is not what governs physics, but rather because *that* it does, and *how* it does, are respectively assumed by, and yet problematic for, every subsequent contribution to the subject.)

One thing is clear, and that is that Benedict shows little sympathy for the distinctly modern thought that the Bible is to be treated as a book of rules. The curious thing about that notion is that, for all its self-proclaimed intention of taking the Bible seriously, it ends up doing no such thing. The point that is worth stressing is this. Rule books, no matter how important, have limited significance in the very sense that we can generally learn to do without them. Take, for example, the rule book (or instruction manual), for using a washing machine. When we first get a washing machine, we may find ourselves referring to the manual all the time. But normally, and usually quite quickly, we do without it. We may keep it in a drawer, just in case – but to all intents and purposes it is done with. Of course, with something much more complicated than a washing machine (such as a nuclear reactor, say), the manual will have a longer shelf life. And we may find it easier, in practice, to rely on it very often, just to save ourselves the trouble of learning it so thoroughly that we can leave it to one side. But in principle we could dispense with it, supposing we worked hard enough.

Now the Bible certainly has some rules – the Ten Commandments most obviously. But significantly Benedict does not treat it as a rule book. Instead, he treats it as if it is, unlike a rule book, utterly indispensable. There is no possibility that one day we could have learnt to do without it. It is to be the monks' daily fare – and not because it contains very many rules and they are slow learners, but rather because it is to provide orientation by which they must direct their lives. It is from the Bible that they must learn to order reality, and they must constantly return to this text to understand themselves and others. They are to allow the Bible, with its confusing mix of chronicles, laws, poems, letters, and stories, to form their imaginations, affections, hopes, and desires. It is to shape their very selves. "Faith," says a modern writer, "is about being apprenticed, trained, exercised, disciplined and formed into a life of faith whose fount and source is the Word of God."[16] Benedict would agree.

Just because Benedict commends this way of using the Bible, Jesus is not placed in that dubious role which much modern Christianity gives to him, as a pre-eminent teacher and source of moral dicta. Christ taught; so much is certain, and Benedict refers to his words, as we have said. But for Benedict, as in the

---

[16] J. Fodor, "Reading the Scriptures: Rehearsing Identity, Practicing Character," in S. Hauerwas and S. Wells, *The Blackwell Companion to Christian Ethics* (Oxford, 2004), 147–8.

Gospels themselves, the description of Jesus as "teacher" (that is, "rabbi"), would indicate a failure to grasp his true significance. Jesus is not only a teacher, and the Bible is not properly understood as a book of teachings. Over the use of the Bible and the significance of Jesus in Christian ethics, differences of emphasis and opinion, rather unsurprisingly, are found in the one and half millennia since Benedict wrote. But Benedict's central concern to make the reading of Scripture, and within that, the telling of the story of Christ, the formative and shaping power in Christian life, has been a dominant theme in the subsequent tradition.

Benedict's guide in reading and interpreting the Bible is Augustine. And so it is to Augustine we must now turn back. For if Benedict has provided us with what we may regard as the paradigmatic form of Christian ethics (with its *what, how,* and *why*), it is Augustine who worked out the basic anthropology (or view of what it is to be human), on which Benedict relies. To put it another way: the *Rule of St Benedict* is the practice of which Augustine's theology is the theory. Thus if we have an answer to the question of the form and character of Christian ethics in the *Rule of St Benedict*, we have nonetheless to step back and see how this paradigmatic answer is itself based in Augustine's deep and wide-ranging reflections on human life under God, and how these reflections themselves were forged in Augustine's lifelong engagement with problems of religious thought and practice.

2

Augustine, God, and Human Nature: The Theory of the Christian Life

What makes an account of the Christian life – a rule for Christian living – compelling? Why does Benedict propose what he does propose and why should anyone else accept it as a guide to how to live?

To call a proposed form of Christian life compelling, so it might be argued, is to say that it is "theo-logical" – that it is a practice which is implied (in the weak and informal sense of "logical"), by Christian teaching concerning God. Saying that God is thus and so – in particular that *this* God, not some general God of philosophical reflection, seeks out and enters into covenant with humanity – it follows that we should live in this or that fashion. So it is that Paul's most lengthy and weighty letter (his Epistle to the Romans), passes from matters of what we might term doctrine to matters of ethics with a "therefore." Having recounted in chapters 1–11 the great narrative of salvation, chapter 12 continues: "Therefore brethren …," and turns to practical matters. It is just because God has done thus and so that we humans are obliged by a "therefore."

What Christianity says about God, and what follows from this for humankind, was and is, however, contested within Christianity, not just from without. And in the period of history before the *Rule*, Christians were appealing to different and competing readings of the Old and New Testaments and their "therefores" were strikingly different: they followed, that is to say, diverse and competing forms of life. Peter Brown's book *The Body and Society* gives a startling account of the variety of ways in which early Christians (i.e. prior to AD 400) thought about celibacy, sex, and asceticism, for example, and of the variety of ways in which they lived and acted in relation to these matters.[1] Some sects disparaged marriage altogether; some thought that marriage itself was permitted, but not second marriage or marriage after the age of childbearing; some thought of childbearing as a duty, whereas others called it in question. Such a variety of beliefs and practices might be found on other issues too – in relation to the legitimacy or otherwise of fleeing from persecution, for example, or on the rights and wrongs of serving in the army, and on the propriety of using doctors in case of illness, and so on. Now within Christianity there would always be diversity, but by the time of the *Rule of St Benedict* there has been a change from the earlier period. For the *Rule* witnesses to – and in turn contributes to – a resolution of contested readings of the story of salvation, a resolution which had key consequences for ethics. This is not to say that there would be no disputes thereafter, and in more or less subtle ways there would be questioning, in theory and in practice, of the resolution to which I refer. But the theological understanding which informs the *Rule of St Benedict* is from this point the touchstone of orthodoxy. And that understanding is the one advanced by Augustine. This is not, it should be said, a historical claim about what Benedict had or hadn't read, but about the source of the theological world view and presuppositions which underlie and make sense of Benedict's prescriptions. Behind Benedict (whether or not he ever glanced over his shoulder), and towering over him, stands Augustine.

Augustine is one of very few theologians whose life would provide promising material for an action-packed Hollywood film. Birth in 354 in North Africa; a powerful, saintly, and rather tearful mother; a (perhaps somewhat exaggerated) wild youth; a seemingly contented relationship with a concubine abandoned for the sake of his career; journeys to the seats of power in the Roman empire in search of fame and fortune; tortured conversions from unbelief to faith, and from one faith

[1]   P. Brown, *The Body and Society: Men, Women and Sexual Renunciation in Early Christianity* (London, 1989).

to another, ending finally in his reception into the church; his struggles as a bishop, once more in North Africa; and his death in 430 as the marauding Vandals reached the very gates of Hippo. Here are the elements for a rip-roaring and visually stunning tale, and, even without the benefit of cinematography, his life has been of abiding interest to subsequent generations. For our purposes, however, we need to attend rather more to his thought than to the events of his life.

From the perspective of the story we are telling, two elements in Augustine's theology are crucial. These two elements were defined and sharpened through his repudiation of two heresies, first the heresy of the Manichees and then the heresy of the Pelagians (though it was Augustine who, in effect, succeeded in getting Pelagianism thus branded). Against the Manichees, Augustine insisted that the world is the work of God and that salvation is thus, to use a slogan, of the world not from it. This element in Augustine's theology is expressed in the *Rule of St Benedict* in what we called the "worldly" character of Christian life as it is there conceived. Against the Pelagians, however, Augustine insisted that the world, though it is indeed the work of God, really does nonetheless need salvation. This salvation, moreover, is a matter not of gaining knowledge but of reordering the will. And it is this element in Augustine's theology which is expressed by Benedict in his insistence that the Christian life is a matter of struggle, challenge, and combat. Thus the character and texture of Christian life – the way of being in the world which the *Rule* teaches for those who follow it – depend crucially on Augustine's moves against these two sets of opponents.

The vast sweep and scope of Augustine's thought is beyond an introduction, but if we are to understand the roots of his influential conception of the shape and character of the Christian life we shall need to take account of these two disputes in turn. And to understand further the practical significance of the resolution of these theological disputes for our "being in the world," we shall consider the bearing of them on Augustine's treatment of a particular set of ethical questions – to do with marriage and sex – as well as on his more general approach to worldly affairs.

Augustine's disputes with Manichees and Pelagians were not unrelated even if we distinguish them and treat them in turn. Both Manichees and Pelagians addressed, in effect, the same question: whence comes evil? The search for an answer to this question constitutes a thread through Augustine's intellectual life, and it was his dissatisfaction with the answers of these two schools of thought and of others which pushed him onwards in his intellectual search, causing him to state, clarify, and refine his own position.

The Manichees reside in that twilight realm reserved for those who have lost important arguments and who are thus known to us chiefly not from their own works – which have generally been suppressed or lost – but largely from the denunciations of the victors (or, as in Augustine's *Confessions*, in the recollections of those who have converted from these, their juvenile errors, and later tell tales of misspent youth). If we lack knowledge of the subtleties and details of the thought of the Manichees, however, we know enough to be clear about the main lines. In general terms, Manichees belong to a group of faiths or philosophies labeled "gnostic," suggesting the arcane knowledge (gnosis), which they claimed to possess and impart as the key to salvation. What is more important for our interests, however, is that, like many gnostics, the Manichees took a dim view of the material world. More strictly, the Manichees were ontological and moral dualists – a dense formulation of a position which is however, happily, quite easily explained.

Ontology has to do with being and dualism with duality or "two-ness." Thus ontological dualism divides the constituents of the realm of being into two – though there are any number of things, so to say, there are, in essence, two ingredients which make up all that is. In both pagan and Christian thought the commonly made distinction was between matter and spirit. This gives us ontological dualism. But besides ontological dualism, many in the ancient world embraced moral dualism. Such dualism not only distinguishes matter and spirit ontologically, but attaches different moral valuations to them. Of course a basic and differential valuation of the two would hold that spirit is somehow better than, or superior to, matter, and this is what many classical and Christian thinkers believed. But the Manichees went further. They didn't just think of spirit as higher than matter, but attached radically different valuations to spirit and matter, and had a theory attributing to them radically different origins. According to these myths, spirit was the work of the true God, and matter was the work of a lesser and inferior God (often identified with the God of the Old Testament, who was not the true God of the New). Evil is the result of our ties to this material realm and salvation consists in the release of spirit from the burden of matter. Matter and spirit are thus not simply distinguished, but in this full-blown moral dualism they are opposed, and this opposition is portrayed in lurid myths of cosmic drama and conflict between competing gods or principles.

Christianity was not without its myths of drama and conflict and salvation, and the Manichees' world view did not wholly lack plausibility – had it done so, Augustine himself would not have been, as he was in his early years, a follower of the Manichees, although never a fully-paid up member. But whatever its initial appeal, Manicheism was finally unsatisfying to Augustine, and that for both philosophical and theological reasons.

Philosophically Augustine was dissatisfied with talk of two gods, or two opposing principles, for the very same reason that the Platonists were; essentially, though this and any other polytheism promised to explain evil, its explanation was arbitrary and mysterious. Why are there *two* gods and why are they locked in endless combat? Monotheism may have its problems, but it has, at least, a certain elegance and simplicity. By contrast, the books of the Manichees were full of "fabulous matters," as Augustine puts it, and those who expounded them were "deceived deceivers" and "word-spinners with nothing to say."[2] Manicheism only "explained" evil by creating other mysteries.

The theological problems with this version of dualism seemed no less real. The Bible might be read and interpreted in many

---

[2]   Augustine, *Confessions*, trans. H. Chadwick (Oxford, 1991), V. x. 19 and VII. ii. 3.

and varied ways, but according to Augustine "the belief that God made the world" has for a "trustworthy witness ... God himself." To know this, we need only turn to the "the holy Scriptures, where his prophet said: 'In the beginning God made heaven and earth.'"[3] To deny that the Bible bears witness to one God, creator and savior, is, to say the least, problematic.

But what has Augustine's dispute with, and repudiation of, Manicheism to do with ethics, you might wonder? Augustine was not the first Christian thinker to see that a belief in God as creator required not only an intellectual but also a practical or moral affirmation of matter. So it is, for example, that we find Clement of Alexandria (writing some 200 years before Augustine), struggling with the question of material possessions in a little sermon known by the title "Who is the rich man that shall be saved?" And Clement struggles for the very reason that he does not allow himself the thought, which would settle the whole issue very quickly, that possessions should be dispensed with for the reason that they are, as belonging to the material realm, bad. Clement has a lot to say about the dangers of possessions and the duties we have in regard to their use. He lays down challenging principles and prescriptions for the wealthy. But that possessions are in and of themselves bad is not one of those principles, nor that we should simply dispose of them one of his general prescriptions.[4]

Our talk of "worldly goods" preserves the decision which early Christianity took at this point – that renunciation may have its reasons, but not the reason that material things are not good, but evil. Christians before and after Clement had understood the need to assert the goodness of the created order and to understand the implications of that belief in day-to-day life. But what that actually meant in practice was by no means clear. Augustine, however, brings to the task of thinking through the practical implications of the belief an immense intellectual

[3]   Augustine, *The City of God*, trans. H. Bettenson (Harmondsworth, 1984), XI. iv.
[4]   Clement's sermon is translated in vol. 2 of the series *The Ante-Nicene Fathers*, repr. in 1994, by T&T Clark, Edinburgh.

power which goes to the very heart of things with unremitting logic. And nowhere do we see this more clearly than in his working out the implications of the repudiation of Manicheism for questions of sexual ethics, which served at the very same time to clarify orthodox thinking. The Manichees' disgust at reproduction arose naturally enough from their disgust at the physical world; but there were, even amongst those who in theory despised their dualism, attitudes towards the physical and the sexual which are barely a step away from that disgust – the views of Augustine's scholarly and ascetic contemporary St. Jerome are a case in point. Jerome would often denounce the Manichees and all their works. But, challenged as to whether he really did believe in the goodness of marriage, he repeated a well-worn classical joke – he always recommended marriage, he said, to those who were frightened of the dark.[5] It was hardly a ringing endorsement and certainly placed little distance between his attitudes and those of the Manichees.

Augustine, however, is clear. Against any disparagement of bodily life and marriage, he insisted on its goodness following especially Jesus's saying in Mark 10: 6–9 ('In the beginning God created man male and female ...') and an increasingly literal reading of Genesis. This reading of Genesis led him to insist that sexual union between man and woman is natural to them as presupposed in their creation in sexual differentiation; he thus rejected not only the views of the Manichees, who denied that God created human beings as man and woman and united them in marriage, but also the views of those such as Gregory of Nyssa, who taught that sexual differentiation and union belonged after the Fall, being made possible by a divine dispensation intended to moderate the bitterness of humankind's punishment by death. Rather, as Augustine insisted in *City of God*, "It is certain that at the beginning male and female were constituted just as two human beings of different sex are now, in our observation and knowledge"; furthermore, even "if there had been no sin, marriage would have been worthy of the

[5] Jerome, *Letters*, 50, in *The Nicene and Post-Nicene Fathers*, 2nd series, vol. 6 (repr. Edinburgh, 1989).

happiness of paradise, and would have given birth to children to be loved."[6] And to make the point even clearer, he maintains that the "actual bodies" to be born in the resurrection will be the bodies of both men and women. "Some people suppose," says Augustine, "that women will not keep their sex at the resurrection." He holds, however, that "the more sensible opinion" is that "there will be both sexes in the resurrection"; for "while all defects will be removed from those bodies, their essential nature will be preserved. Now a woman's sex is not a defect; it is natural" – thereby renouncing Aristotle's view of the nature of the female sex as a failed male. "He who established the two sexes will restore them both," insists Augustine, for the sexes are both good.[7]

Augustine was clear and could hardly have been any clearer – and there was no topic on which to make the Christian embrace of the world more stark. The very bodies we have, the bodies of men and women as we know them, are created by God and will persist in the resurrection. And notice that this thorough repudiation of the dualism of the Manichees is just as thorough a repudiation of the half-hearted dualism of the pagan or classical world, and of those Christians who were unduly influenced by it. If classical thinkers disparaged, as they did, notions of competing gods or principles, nonetheless they still regarded the material as a sort of weight holding down the spirit and something which we had to rise above, and which in salvation, however conceived, would be thrown off. Jokes need not be based wholly on truth to be funny, but they must have a degree of plausibility – and there is just such plausibility in the story of the great pagan philosopher Porphyry, a contemporary of Augustine, bursting into tears when food was placed in front of him since it reminded him that he had a body as well as a soul.

By contrast, Augustine is thoroughly worldly. He insists that the world is the work of God and that salvation is thus, to repeat that slogan, of the world not from it. We cannot simply run away from the material and we cannot despise it. It may be

6   *City of God*, XIV. xxiii.
7   *City of God*, XXII. xvii.

that in the use of the material we need to exercise care and restraint in various ways. But this is not because the material world is evil or merely a distraction – it is rather because we need to use it aright. What is striking here is the insistence that we can and indeed must find good in this sphere, for worldly goods really are goods.

This, as we said in the last chapter, is a lesson which Benedict had learnt well. The monk, it will be recalled, is charged with serving God and neighbor, and serving the latter in the very stuff of life, through work, and through the provision of food, shelter, and care. We referred to this as the worldliness of the monastery – not the worldliness which would be the object of critiques of the decadent monasticism of later times, but the worldliness which sees the world as the scene and subject of God's salvation. The monk is not to turn his back on the world, but, in various ways, is to cherish and serve it.

Augustine's answer to the Manichees had practical implications. But for a moment we need to return to the theoretical adequacy of that answer if we are to understand the full significance of Augustine's theology for ethics. Remember that the dualism of the Manichees pretended to offer an explanation of evil. Evil results from matter and matter is to be repudiated. According to Augustine, this solution is unsatisfactory for both philosophical and theological reasons. Matter is not evil nor even the cause of evil. Rather, the world as God created it is good. Still, however, the world in which we live is plainly not in any simple and unqualified way good – the Manichees were not mistaken in finding evil in the world, only mistaken in their explanation of its source. If the Manichees' solution to the problem of evil is wrong, the problem still remains. What then is the origin or source of the evil which only too plainly afflicts a world which is, in its origins and source, supposedly good?

In answering this question, and in characterizing and understanding more fully the nature of salvation, Augustine did battle with another set of opponents, the Pelagians. In certain respects the Pelagians are as shadowy as the Manichees, but what seems to have motivated their thought was something which Augustine would have regarded as wholly admirable, and that was a determination to avoid the errors of the Manichees. The Pelagians were determined, that is to say, not to locate evil or its source in an ontology – that is, in a theory of being, matter, or nature. Rather, they maintained resolutely that nature was good – including human nature. Sin and evil did not, then, arise from this nature as if it belonged to it, but was rather a question of this nature's misuse. So, according to Peter Brown, the Pelagian view was that though "the powers of human nature had, admittedly, been constricted by the weight of past habits and by the corruption of society," "such constriction was purely superficial."[8] Thus, since the burden of sexual sins for example, as of any others, was a burden of habit and imitation and not a burden attached to our very natures, it could be shaken off with more or less ease. To suppose otherwise, so leading Pelagians would say – to suppose, that is, that we are freighted with more than the weight of bad habits and bad examples – is simply to fall back in with the Manichees in their disparage-ment of the world, and in so doing to encourage the moral laxity and torpor which come about when we allow ourselves to say "I couldn't" when honestly we ought only to say "I didn't." As Pelagius explained in his *Letter to Demetrius*, God has made human nature and knows its capabilities – since perfection is possible, it is obligatory.

To Augustine this answer to the problem of evil seemed shal-low. True enough, he would say, the Manichees attack "human nature" with "detestable censure"; yet the Pelagians on the other side heap on human nature what he calls "cruel praise."[9] The Pelagians, in other words, say all sorts of good things about human nature (and thus are better than the Manichees), but this "praise" is "cruel" for the very reason that they don't take at all seriously the gravity of the situation in which we find our-selves, imagining that we can save ourselves with a bit of effort.

[8]   P. Brown, *Augustine of Hippo* (London, 1967), 365.
[9]   Augustine, *On Marriage and Concupiscence*, trans. P. Holmes and R. Wallis, *Nicene and Post-Nicene Fathers*, 1st series, vol. 5 (Edinburgh, 1991), ii. 9.

But saving ourselves with a bit of effort was not true to Augustine's experience or understanding. His most compelling account of the human predicament is, it might seem, a work of self-analysis, for the description of this predicament as consisting in the division of the will against itself is most memorably presented in Book VIII of his own *Confessions*:

> As I deliberated about serving my Lord God which I had long been disposed to do, the self which willed to serve was identical with the self which was unwilling. It was I. I was neither wholly willing nor wholly unwilling. So I was in conflict with myself and was dissociated from myself. The dissociation came about against my will.[10]

This is, of course, a conscious echo of Paul's lament in his Epistle to the Romans about the good he would, but could not, do, and the evil he would not, but did, do! Augustine means this, then, not as self-analysis; his "I" is a human, not a personal, one. The human predicament does not lie, as the Manichees suppose, in the need to escape matter, though there is indeed a predicament. It is our inability to will the good, in that division of the self against the self in which we are at war with ourselves, willing even that which we do not want to will. We should master evil, but evil masters us, so that we are incapable of that wholeness and purity which belong to us in our proper state. Certainly we do not need to escape the world, but we need more than Pelagian exhortation if we are to live in it well. We are wounded and cannot make ourselves whole and healthy; we need to be saved and healed by God's grace.

But if this is our predicament in relation to evil, how did it come about? Our being wounded in our natures is, says Augustine, a result of the Fall. God did not create us in this fallen state in which we are at war in ourselves and incapable of willing the good. God created us good. And yet Adam sinned. Why? Simply out of pride, according to Augustine – Adam was placed in a garden and was commanded by God not to eat of

---

[10] *Confessions*, VIII. x. 22.

one single tree in a garden filled with trees bearing all that was good to eat. A less demanding command there could not have been. So not out of hunger or need, but simply out of pride, Adam rebelled. He could not bear, speculates Augustine, that he should be anything other than a law to himself. And he who would not be governed was punished by being incapable of governing even himself – a fitting punishment, transmitted as a wound to the entire human race.

It is worth noting that pride, the root of the sin which turned man against God, is also, according to Augustine, the root of the sin which turns man against man. If Adam, in his pride, had to be autonomous (a law to himself), even against God, it was certain that he would not suffer the command or rule of another. What turned man against God would also turn him against the other, explaining the disorder of earthly life as much as the disorder in human and divine relations. Thus what in the *Confessions* might seem to be an analysis of the individual human condition becomes, in the monumental and magisterial work the *City of God*, a basis for a history of the world and for a critique of the politics of the Roman empire. Just as his own life and history could be read in terms of the struggle of the self to will well or badly, so could the life and history of the world be read in terms of a conflict between "two cities ... created by two kinds of love." The one city, the earthly city, is "created by self-love reaching the point of contempt for God, the Heavenly City by the love of God carried as far as contempt for self."[11] For all the pretence of virtue, what finally lies behind the glory of Rome is the self-love and the pride which seek to rule rather than to be ruled, or even to share rule. Adam's prideful turn against God is in its essence a turn against the other, and thus the root of the discord between man and man, as well as between man and God.

The doctrine of the Fall is meant to provide a solution to the problem of evil, and to find a way between the Manichees and the Pelagians. It holds to the view that salvation is of the world,

[11]   *City of God*, XIV. xxviii.

not from it, whilst also insisting that the world, though it is good in its origins and substance, really does need salvation. And Augustine holds to this line by asserting the existence not of a dualism of substance, being, or nature, but rather of a deep and far from trivial disorder. The drama of salvation results, so we might say, not from a world which is wrongly constituted, but from a will which is wrongly directed. So the battle is not, as for the Manichees, with an evil which is other and elsewhere, but with an evil which is here and mine, the evil of the disordered and divided self. It is the will, not that from which we are made, which turns us from the good and from God. It is the will which is rotten or – to use Augustine's term – fallen. According to Augustine, "Man's nature owes nothing to the Devil. But, by persuading man to sin, the Devil violated what God made well, so that the whole human race limps because of the wound made through the free choice of two human beings."[12] Thus,

> man's safety and the salvation of his nature consists in this, not that the flesh and the spirit, as though by nature hostile to each other as the Manichaean foolishly thinks, may be separated, but that they may [contrary to what the Pelagian deems necessary] be healed of the fault of discord and be in harmony.[13]

Manichees are wrong to think the flesh evil, whereas Pelagians are wrong to think it is not disordered or that its ills are of such a kind that we can ourselves, by our willpower, accomplish our deliverance. We cannot. And specifically we cannot do the good without the assistance of divine grace to release us from that discord in which we cannot will wholly and well. Salvation we certainly need; but from discord, not from nature.

Here, then, in Augustine's powerful thought – so powerful that it would dominate the Christian world for ever after – we have the theory which gives birth to the practice which is

[12]   Augustine, *Contra Julianum*, trans. M. A. Schumacher (Washington, 1957), iv. 16. 83.
[13]   *Contra Julianum*, ii. 3. 6.

commended and presented by Benedict. Benedict refers to the monastery as a school, but it is a funny sort of school. Schools in our modern understanding are places where the immature go for a time to gain knowledge and skills. But the pupils in Benedict's school enter not to gain knowledge, but to do battle. The battle is with the self, the aim is to learn obedience, the weapon is humility, and success is a gift and not an accomplishment. Salvation is not, in other words, a matter of acquiring further information, nor of gaining a skill, but of winning a conflict – and a conflict not as the Manichees may have allowed with an evil which is other and elsewhere, but with an evil which is here and mine, the evil of the disordered and divided self. And, let us underline the point, the conflict is not concluded, but is ongoing; this school has no graduates, only lifelong pupils.

It was one of Augustine's key contributions to the self-understanding of Christianity – and in turn to the self-definition of Christianity against paganism – that *the* moral problem is the problem of the will. This is a presupposition which has come down as a part of our Western heritage, and countless modern novels make the same presupposition without, perhaps, knowing that this way of seeing things has a certain particularity.

But, quite consciously for Augustine, this way of conceiving the situation involved a turn away from the classical tradition. Classical ethics had proposed a view of the good life from which Christians borrowed and learnt in subtle and complex ways. But Christianity deepened and darkened the whole subject of ethics by proposing that the problem of how to be human was a problem not chiefly of knowledge, but of will. Aristotle had complained of Socrates that "he thought all the virtues were forms of knowledge."[14] And Christianity would make a similar complaint not just against Socrates, but against the classical tradition in general, and it followed its own quite different path.

Whatever problems there may be with the doctrine of the Fall as a causal account of the human condition – and Augustine's

[14]   Aristotle, *The Eudemian Ethics*, trans. H. Rackham (London, 1952), I. v. 15.

contemporaries pressed many problems against it, in particular the question of the very possibility of the transmission of Adam's disability to his descendants, let alone the justice of such a punishment – psychologically it is powerful and persuasive, leaving other accounts looking shallow and slight. This is nowhere clearer, to stick with the example discussed in regard to the Manichees, than in relation to sex.

The power of Augustine's account of the human condition, against that favored by the Pelagians, is just that it does not represent the human problem in this sphere as that of simply making good or bad choices. True enough this may represent part of the challenge, but does not exhaust it, for in this realm we face not difficult choices but inclinations, traits, and drives which threaten to, and sometimes do, enthrall us, so that our actions can appear to us hardly like choices at all. I may choose to park on double yellow lines believing I will get away with it; I may choose not to be fully honest in filling out my tax return calculating that I am unlikely to be found out. But we will not come to terms with certain phenomena in human sexual life – amongst them the awfully widespread phenomena of child abuse, rape, addiction to pornography, and the like – if "bad choices" remains our principal analytic tool. We shall never come to terms with these phenomena, that is to say, while we think that "choosing better" is the solution to our predicament; our real predicament lies in enthrallment to bad choices and thus in an inability to choose well.

The thought that we are in our natures wounded or fallen is one which makes sense not only of our experience in this particular sphere, but more widely too. From Augustine's time on, the conviction that the moral problem of humankind is not simply one of gaining knowledge and choosing well, but the altogether deeper and more intractable problem of a self subject to powerful and conflicting forces, has held an immense power. We could trace this sense of self through the psychology expressed in music and painting, in prayers and hymns, in novels and poetry – in the nineteenth and twentieth centuries we find it in Tolstoy and Dostoevsky and Zola and Conrad, as well as in Freud and those who have learnt from him. The analysis of this problem is various and diverse, but at its core Western psychology has derived from a diagnosis given such powerful form in the anguish of *The Confessions*, where Augustine painted a picture of a self which could not be saved by the glib moralism of the Pelagians.

Augustine is a great theorist of human nature and the human condition, but he was not only a theorist. Though the volume of his theological works may belie the fact, as a bishop Augustine was, on a daily basis, much pressed by practical and pastoral concerns of a diverse and demanding character. In virtue of his being a bishop in the late Roman empire, Augustine was possessed of civic responsibilities, and he had authority as a judge in certain matters, and the authority to counsel, advise, and influence in countless others. Thus, as one commentator puts it, as a "committed protagonist in a compassionless civil society ... [Augustine] may appear to us to be in a perilous situation."[15]

What is of interest, however, is how Augustine coped with this "perilous situation," informed as he was by the theological understanding we have outlined – a theological understanding which casts a sense of melancholy over the world and its life, for this life is subject to the flaws which afflict humanity. The result is a practice which from a Pelagian point of view might seem pessimistic, but from another exhibits a realistic and modest hopefulness for social life. As Atkins and Dodaro put it:

> Augustine's pastoral writings do not include clear-cut and systematic political theory, but they are underpinned by a consistent and coherent view of humanity and society. On the basis of this he tackles fundamental questions of political authority in the form of concrete practical problems. Sometimes, this leads him to articulate uncompromising principles; more often, he allows Christian ideals such as mercy to put whatever pressure they can on the social structures of a fallen world.[16]

---

[15]   S. Lancel, *St Augustine*, trans. A. Nevill (London, 2002), 268.
[16]   Augustine, *Political Writings*, ed. E. M. Atkins and R. J. Dodaro (Cambridge, 2001), p. xxvii.

"Putting pressure on a fallen world" has none of the glamour of revolution, nor the satisfying purity of a sulky and pessimistic withdrawal; arguably, however, it is the proper and characteristic form of Christian endeavor in promoting human being in the earthly city. And Augustine worked out what this entailed, in many and difficult circumstances.

In the matter of slavery for example – clearly for Augustine a social structure belonging to a "fallen world" – this approach can seem to modern eyes highly uncomfortable. In one of his letters (Epistle 10) Augustine is concerned with certain illegal practices in the obtaining and selling of slaves; but the letter contains nothing to suggest a critique of slavery as such (but only of "the cowboys in the trade" as Garnsey puts it[17]), and involves an appeal for the moderation of the severe punishments designated for irregular traders. As to opposing slavery in itself, "it never occurs to Augustine that slavery might be abolished" and his efforts "were directed to goals that were limited and achievable"[18] – specifically the end of abuses of the then current institution of slavery rather than the end of the institution itself.

In relation to corporal and capital punishment there is, likewise, an acceptance of the necessity of the practices, while at the same time Augustine requires of those whom he petitions that they allow mercy, in need of which we all stand, to exercise a tempering influence. As Lancel notes: "the bishop would make efforts to cheat the executioner of his victims, but would not dream of rendering him definitively unemployed."[19] He would mitigate the severity of punishment where he could, but he never expected that the world would get by without it.

If, however, we are to understand Augustine's principled, albeit patient and modest, interventions in the life of the earthly city, it is vital to notice that, alongside these, another element of social engagement and critique is to be found in the monastic

[17]   P. Garnsey, *Ideas of Slavery from Aristotle to Augustine* (Cambridge, 1996), 63.
[18]   Augustine, *Political Writings*, ed. Atkins and Dodaro, p. xxvi.
[19]   Lancel, *St Augustine*, 269.

practices which he shaped and sponsored. It is important to say "monastic practices," for these went wider than what we might think of as regular monastic observance, from which Augustine was removed on taking up the full responsibilities of a bishop. These more informal observances included the establishing of his own residence as a *monasterium clericorum*: a community for the clergy of Hippo, who were obliged "to surrender all their possessions, to the benefit of the church of Hippo or another church, or in favour of their own families if the situation demanded it, to have bed and board with their bishop, and be fed and clothed at the community's expense."[20] In this surrender of possessions, rigorously enforced, we can hardly fail to notice a "social intervention" rather different in character from the "patient and modest" pressure found elsewhere; indeed, the practice of monasticism speaks of a more impatient hope and a more urgent pressing forward than witnessed in Augustine's day-to-day dealings with officials, soldiers, and magistrates. Taken together, but not apart, his activity in the two spheres expresses something of the character of Christian hope for redeemed human life, no matter its fallen condition.

We have already seen Benedict's attempt to translate Augustine's understanding of humanity in relation to God into a way of being in the world. This way of being is worldly, but otherworldly; melancholy and hopeful; critical, yet patient. It arises from a sustained and profound struggle to make sense of the world, and expresses a deep and persistent engagement with it. Together Augustine and Benedict provide Christianity's paradigmatic answer to the question of ethics, and one which would exert a huge influence. Across Europe, communities would be formed which would incorporate these ideas into their daily life, and in this life bear witness to a particular conception of what it is to live well. A Roman thinker from before the Common Era, transported to the beginning of the sixth century, would reckon that the moral world which he or she had known had many continuities with this newly conceived world.

[20]   Lancel, *St Augustine*, 229.

And the same might be said by a Jewish thinker too. Marriage was still honored. Theft was still punished. Lying was still frowned upon. But in subtle ways, attitudes to life and death, to the body and property, to celibacy and childbearing, to punishment and charity, had all been touched by the particular understanding of God and humankind which early Christian thinkers had imbibed from the story of Christ.

3

Thomas Aquinas: Natural Law and the Loss of Christian Ethics

It is not given to writers to determine the reception and the use, and hence the fate, of their works. The forces which determine these things are highly various and for the most part outside a writer's control. So it is that few would be happy to own the -isms which have been named after them. Thomas Aquinas is no exception; it seems highly unlikely that he would welcome the transformation of his thought into Thomism. One commentator puts it more strongly: "We have witnessed the decapitation of Aquinas."[1]

Very few -isms, however, are simply utter travesties of the thought of their originators. Thus if the seven hundred and more years which have passed since Thomas's death in 1274 have seen developments of his thought which he would not welcome, it is nonetheless true that Thomism took a direction from Thomas himself. Thomism might be seen as going further than Thomas intended – but the direction in which it moves is one in which he was traveling.

What is this direction? One of the tags or slogans which is often used to capture and convey a central theme or emphasis of Thomas's thought is that "grace perfects nature." God's grace, that is to say, brings nature to completion. It does not lay on top of nature a set of arbitrary or foreign demands, but rather allows nature to achieve its fulfillment. Thomas finds, then, a continuity in the operation of salvation, not a rupture or a disjunction. Thus he is inclined to minimize the distance or contrast between the unfallen, fallen, and redeemed worlds.

[1] S. Pinkaers, *Sources of Christian Ethics*, trans. M. T. Noble (Edinburgh, 1995), 171.

Nowhere is this clearer than in his account of political society where, as we shall see, Thomas takes a significantly different approach to that favored by Augustine. The same sense of harmony rather than disjunction is found in another central and influential element within his body of thought, and that is in his confidence in the harmony of reason and faith. The question of whether and how Thomism goes beyond Thomas will be posed precisely here – for what is characteristic of Thomism, but perhaps not of Thomas, is a confidence not only in the harmony of reason and faith, but in the power of reason to warrant fundamental beliefs about God and, most importantly for the interests of this book, to warrant beliefs about morality.

Suggestive of the tenor or direction of Thomas's thought is his disagreement with Augustine on the matter of the origins of political authority. Thomas believes that the very existence of human society requires the exercise of political authority, whereas Augustine held that political authority became necessary only with the Fall. God declares, says Augustine, " 'Let him have lordship over the fish of the sea, the birds of the sky … and all the reptiles that crawl on the earth'. He did not wish the rational beings, made in his own image, to have dominion over any but irrational creatures, not man over man, but man over beasts. Hence the first just men were set up as shepherds of flocks, rather than as kings of men."[2]

According to Augustine, then, the use of coercive power was a providential institution designed to preserve a minimal peace in a sinful world. Thomas, however, believes that the rule of some over others belongs to mankind's natural condition. Thus in chapter 1 of his early work "On Princely Government," having rehearsed arguments which demonstrate that "the fellowship of society" is "natural and necessary to man" – a point with which Augustine would have agreed – he continues:

> it follows with equal necessity that there must be some principle of government within the society. For if a great number of people were to live, each intent upon his own interests, such a community

---

[2]   Augustine, *City of God*, XIX. xv.

would surely disintegrate unless there were one of its number to have a care for the common good: just as the body of a man or of any other animal would disintegrate were there not in the body itself a single and controlling force, sustaining the general vitality of all the members. As Solomon tells us (Prov xi, 14): "Where there is no ruler the people shall be scattered." This conclusion is quite reasonable; for the particular interest and the common good are not identical.[3]

It is this last which is the important and central point. Society has a good which is not the sum of individual goods or "particular interests" – just as does a team or an army, for example. And because this is so, the exercise of political authority is not simply a regrettable expedient as a result of sin, but a natural necessity of social life, and one which aims at a positive, not a negative, good: not simply the restraint of chaos and disorder (expressed chiefly in keeping the peace and punishing evildoers), but the achievement of a common good. The point, then, is that according to Thomas "government would be required even if there were no evildoers and even if no one was inclined to break the peace."[4] As he says elsewhere: "The control of one over another who remains free, can take place when the former directs the latter to his own good or to the common good. And such dominion would have been found between man and man in the state of innocence."[5] As society is natural to humankind, so too is the institution of authority within it, as that without which society could not realize its proper end and form.

With this apparently small transfer of political authority from after to before the Fall, there is a major shift of mood and expectation. What Augustine seems to lament as an albeit necessary expedient, Aquinas regarded as intrinsic to human life in society. It is worth noting, of course, that this rationale and

[3]   *Aquinas: Selected Political Writings*, ed. A. P. D'Entrèves, trans. J. G. Dawson (Oxford, 1959), 3.
[4]   F. C. Copleston, *Aquinas* (Harmondsworth, 1955), 229.
[5]   Aquinas, *Summa Theologiae*, 1a2ae, 96, 4; these and subsequent quotations are from vol. 28 of the Blackfriars edition, trans. T. Gilby (London, 1966).

justification of political authority, while it seems to replace Augustine's concession with a more positive appreciation, is not a simple or blanket vindication of political power and its exercise. In fact it suggests important limits to the exercise of political authority, something which Thomas draws out especially in his treatment of law. We shall turn to that in due course, but we should note that the purpose of authority is to allow society to achieve the common good, so that such authority is wrongly exercised where it does not serve this end. Thus the basis for the appreciation of political authority is at the very same time the basis for a critique of its exercise. These two elements have been characteristic of Roman Catholic social ethics down to our own time: according a dignity to political authority provides at the same time the platform or basis for a critique.

We might think of Thomas's treatment of the issue of political authority as emblematic; it is suggestive of the direction of his thought, which lies towards stressing the continuities between nature and grace and the sense in which the latter works with the grain of the former, not against it. A central element in Thomas's thought which supports this continuity, as we have already mentioned, is his confidence in the harmony of reason and faith.

In the newly emerging universities of the thirteenth century, and in the university of Paris at which Thomas taught, the relationship of faith and reason was a central intellectual problem. The faith which was in question was the Christian faith as understood by Augustine; Augustine's intellectual power and scope made him the pre-eminent and presiding authority over Christian thought for the whole of the early Middle Ages (that is, from his death in 430 until the thirteenth century). That is not to say that, were we drawing a map to a larger scale, there would be no other landmarks to note: Gregory the Great, Anselm of Canterbury, and Bernard of Clairvaux, for example, are, in their different ways, figures of great influence and interest. It is, nonetheless, Augustine who provided the understanding and explication of Christianity which shaped the faith of the Middle Ages down to the thirteenth century (and, of course, beyond).

Now the reason which this faith encountered was a reason which had been learnt from the newly rediscovered works of Aristotle. Aristotle had been lost to the Latin West, and his thought only returned in translation from Arabic, from the great centers of Islamic philosophy such as Cordoba. What was discovered in Aristotle was not only a wide-ranging and powerful body of thought wholly independent of Christianity, but one which seemed, at the very least, to put questions to it. For example, the Bible seems to teach that the world has a beginning in time, whereas Aristotle holds that, for all we know, the world may be eternal.

This particular meeting of faith and reason was seen by some as a matter of either/or: either one could choose Augustine (and be suspected of fideism, the view that religious belief is wholly a matter of faith and not of reason), or one could be a partisan of the new philosophy (and be of doubtful orthodoxy). Thomas refuses this either/or and instead seeks a harmony between faith and reason. The very structure of the monumental work for which Thomas is chiefly remembered, the *Summa Theologiae*, bespeaks this intention.

The *Summa* is organized thematically as a modern work might be, but the treatment of each and every theme is organized through the discussion of a series of questions – for example, the discussion of law asks whether law is a function of reason, whether it is ordained for the common good, whether anybody can make law, and so on. Now the treatment of each question typically begins with a clash of claims, ideas, reasons, or authorities. It seems that such and such is the case as, say, Augustine, Jerome, or whoever, holds. On the other hand, it seems that such and such is not the case, for whatever reason, as Aristotle, or St. Paul, or the book of Deuteronomy contend. But this clash is not left as a clash, and very rarely does Thomas make a simple choice for one side over the other; instead, in the discussion which follows the presentation of the opposed views, Thomas typically offers a synthesis which overcomes or resolves the seemingly sharp disagreement. And, so it might be said, the structure of this work is a sign of the structure or character of Thomas's wider intellectual undertaking – where his contemporaries find contradiction between Augustine and Aristotle, Thomas finds a synthesis. Aristotle can embrace Christianity, and Christianity can embrace Aristotle. It is not a matter choosing faith or reason, but of affirming both.

If confidence in the essential harmony of reason and faith is a key aspect of Thomas's thought, Thomism is marked, we might say, by a further step, and that is a confidence in the power of reason alone to warrant fundamental beliefs about God and morality. Unaided human reason can, according to Thomism, tell us certain things about God's existence and nature – the so-called Five Ways ("There are five ways in which one can prove that there is a God") provide a starting point in Thomas's writing for the development of what is known as natural theology. In addition, so Thomism holds, human reason can, without appeal to theological premises and presuppositions, tell us certain things about what is good and bad, and where our duties lie. For Thomism such reasoning concerns the natural law, and here Thomism took as its fount and source just a few pages in the vast *Summa* where Thomas discusses that topic. And what specifically, does such reasoning tell us? It was, and of course remains, a contentious issue. We shall come presently to what Thomas himself seems to have thought on the matter. But it is perhaps certain of the papal encyclicals of the nineteenth and twentieth centuries which represent the most vaunting claims for the power of unaided reason in this sphere, holding as they do that, amongst other things, abortion, divorce, contraception, dueling, homosexuality, and euthanasia are all contrary to the natural law, and that they are known to be wrong on the basis of reason alone.

The question of whether Thomism goes beyond Thomas, albeit in the same direction, is less interesting, of course, than the question of the plausibility of the claims made by Thomism about the power of reason to establish substantial ethical principles. To judge the plausibility of that claim, we must look at those few pages of the *Summa* relating to the natural law in the way that Thomism looked at them, that is, as essentially self-contained; we shall not be concerned, in the first instance, to relate this discussion to the wider context of Thomas's theology.

Instead we shall consider what these few pages are said to teach about the natural law, its scope and power, noting only in passing that the centrality of natural law for Thomism is in contrast to the limited place of the natural law in Thomas's thinking. And we will cast some doubts on the pretensions of Thomism to establish ethics on the basis of reason alone. In advancing our history, we will find it helpful to address the question as to why Thomism displaced Thomas – why, that is, the relatively brief treatment of natural law, removed from its context, eclipsed his own teaching with its seemingly quite different character and purpose.

On the subject of natural law, Thomas declares that "the natural law is nothing other than the sharing in the Eternal Law by intelligent creatures"[6] – which leads us to wonder, what is the Eternal Law, and what is it to share in it? The Eternal Law is, so to speak, the divine blueprint existing in the mind of God, according to which all things are as they are. But different things are directed to the attainment of their ends in different ways; or, to use his language, different things participate differently in the Eternal Law. Some things are subject to this law "by way of being acted upon and acting from having received from it an inner principle of motion."[7] So it is with acorns, copper, water, bees, and so on: acorns grow into oaks, copper conducts electricity, water boils at 100 degrees, and bees gather honey – and they do so because this belongs to their nature, or, as we say, because of the laws of nature. But there is another way of "being subject to the Eternal Law," and that is by "being a companion by way of knowledge,"[8] and this belongs to rational creatures. All things are ruled by the "eternal law" in that "their tendencies to their own proper acts and ends are from its impression," but in addition (that is, as well as having these tendencies), rational creatures can "join in and make their own the Eternal Reason" through knowledge and understanding. Through knowledge and understanding, that is to say, rational

[6]   *Summa Theologiae*, 1a2ae, 90, 2.
[7]   *Summa Theologiae*, 1a2ae, 93, 6.
[8]   Ibid.

beings may make the law of their being their own, willing to be what they are directed to be by their nature; "natural law," says Thomas, "is promulgated by God's so instilling it into men's minds that they can know it because of what they really are."[9] And this is what it is to share in the Eternal Law – to know for oneself, by using one's intelligence, what belongs to one's nature. To know this is to know the natural law.

But what do humans know by sharing in the Eternal Law, by knowing what "they really are"? In broad terms, says Thomas, we know three things. First, that we share an inclination with all creatures to preserve ourselves in existence. Thus the natural law directs us, says Thomas, "to maintain and defend the elementary requirements of human life" – that is, it commands us to do those things which preserve and protect life and health. Secondly,

> there is in man a bent towards things which accord with his nature considered more specifically, that is, in terms of what he has in common with other animals; correspondingly those matters are said to be of natural law which nature teaches all animals, for instance the coupling of male and female, the bringing up of the young, and so forth.

And then in the third place, there is what belongs to us not just as creatures or animals, but specifically as humans; that is, "there is in man an appetite for the good of his nature as rational"; thus:

> it is proper to him ... that he should know the truths about God and about living in society. Correspondingly, whatever this involves is a matter of natural law, for instance that a man should shun ignorance, not offend others with whom he ought to live in civility, and other such related requirements.[10]

And with that rather throw-away ending to the sentence ("... and other such related requirements"), Thomas seems to let the

[9] *Summa Theologiae*, 1a2ae, 90, 4.
[10] *Summa Theologiae*, 1a2ae, 94, 2.

matter drop. He has told us what the natural law is: it is to know what belongs to our nature as human beings, through the exercise of our intelligence or reason. And he has indicated, in the broadest terms, what sort of things belong to our nature: preserving ourselves in existence, caring for our offspring, seeking to know God and to live in society with others. But if one asks what more precisely and specifically does this law provide, one can only say that, as far as we can tell, Thomas is uninterested in the question. Certainly he says nothing to give much encouragement to the Thomist project of advancing a set of moral principles and precepts warranted by unaided reason. Indeed, according to one contemporary commentator:

> There is only one sustained discussion, extending over several articles, in which Thomas subjects a disputed issue of personal conduct to what could be called a natural law analysis.... Interestingly, the problem [of polygamy] was one which he could not resolve by using natural law. Thomas ends up saying that polygamy violates no first precept of the natural law. With the ordering of sex to procreation, the polygamist does not violate the natural law. The remainder of Thomas's argument was a tentative one, namely, that polygamy made social life inconvenient and that it would be difficult for the society of husband and wife to maintain itself properly intact in that kind of arrangement. His only decisive argument against polygamy is sacramental – Jesus cannot have plural churches, man cannot have plural wives. And so the one serious effort he made to resolve the kind of issue we talk about today – a disputed moral issue – ended somewhat inconclusively on the natural law note.[11]

In fact, when we revert to the section of Thomas's work we were discussing, the only thing to be gleaned are the reasons for thinking that natural law will not take us very far at all in our moral reasoning; thus, one of the reasons why God gives divine law (such as is found in the Old and New Testaments), is "the

---

[11] R. Hittenger, "Natural Law and Catholic Moral Theology," in M. Cromartie, ed., *A Preserving Grace* (Washington, 1997), 8.

untrustworthiness of human judgment."[12] Furthermore, both of the ways in which we share in the Eternal Law "are imperfect and, as it were, decayed in the wicked: their natural instinct for virtue is spoilt by vice and their natural knowledge of what is right is darkened by the passions and habits of sin."[13]

This hesitancy about the power and ability of reasoning from the natural law to solve our moral problems was not shared by Thomism. According to Thomism, as we have noted, a whole host of things are said to be known to be wrong, by the light of the natural law. But what are we to make of this contention? Whether or not it is a contention which goes beyond Thomas, how plausible is it? What can we expect such arguments to establish and achieve? Will they, for example, teach us the wrongness of homosexuality, abortion, divorce, the use of contraception and the like?

Without reviewing each of those claims in turn to see how far argument can get us, we might offer the following maxim: that the claims of natural law are, where uncontroversial, uninteresting and where interesting, controversial. Take, for example, the claim that it is wrong to kill. Most people, at most times and in most places, would sign a petition in support of such a contention. But the various people who sign, so we would be bound to note, have had some very different practices in relation to killing. Some of them would expose unwanted children; some put the aged outside the camp to fend for themselves; some will engage in ethnic cleansing; some will practice euthanasia; some will allow abortion on demand; some will make use of capital punishment; some will believe in total war; and some will be pacifists. Thus the claim that killing is wrong is one which wins wide support while leaving unsettled the very issues which most concern us – and on these issues, the claim to establish such and such a conclusion as demanded by reason would be highly contentious. It is not impossible that natural reasoning may bring about agreement, or move us towards agreement on all sorts of issues, and the particular claims can

[12] *Summa Theologiae*, 1a2ae, 91, 4.
[13] *Summa Theologiae*, 1a2ae, 93, 6.

only be tested by examination of the particular arguments – but the notion that reasoning and argument will deliver a highly interesting set of propositions seems belied by the sort of moral disagreement which rages between Christians, let alone more widely still. The question of the scope and power of reason in ethics will concern us in later chapters, but here we may simply note that broad agreement across societies and times in formulating certain rules as necessary for facilitating common life may be important and worthy of remark; but it obviously doesn't constitute a sufficient basis for agreement on the more detailed texture of moral life.

Certainly Thomas himself did not regard the moral law as the center of things; his treatment of the natural law was not meant to be taken in isolation, nor to provide the basis for a complete moral theology. His moral theology in fact comprises the whole of the second part of the *Summa*, of which the treatment of law in general is but a very small part. Thomas argues that happiness is the end of human life, and that happiness consists in life with God. The principles or causes of our going towards God he divides as internal or external. The internal or subjective springs or principles of our actions are the virtues, which are themselves perfected by the gifts of the Holy Spirit. The external or objective principles of our actions are law and grace. These together move us towards our end in God.

Seen in this context the insistence on the naturalness of the natural law is not intended chiefly to make an epistemological point (i.e. about what we can know of this law), but rather to stress the continuity of nature and grace. We have our origin in God and we return to God, and the return to God which virtue, law, and grace together accomplish is not a wrenching and twisting of our humanity, but a matter of our being liberated from the perversion of sin, which prevents our realizing ourselves and our true ends. Thomas's thought, but not Thomism, is theological through and through, notwithstanding the fact that it owes much to Aristotle.

If this is so, how is it, we might wonder, that Thomism so mistook Thomas that he is barely recognizable in the thought which claimed his name? To explain this we need to look backwards and forwards, an exercise which will serve to fill in slightly the history of Christian ethics up to this point and also to lead us on to the next installment.

Looking backwards, we have noticed already that the move from Augustine to Thomas Aquinas involves our leaping over some eight hundred years. And we have noted too that in a more detailed treatment there are writers to whom we would wish to refer – such as Gregory the Great and Bernard of Clairvaux. However that may be, it remains true that the authority of Augustine is so overwhelming that there is no one figure whom we absolutely have to notice (in a brief history) before we notice Thomas Aquinas.

But if there is no single writer who demands our attention, there is a development which does: one which was significant not only for the reception of Thomas's thought, but also for determining the path of moral theology up to and, especially in the Roman Catholic tradition, beyond the Reformation. The development in question was the spread of the practice of auricular confession (i.e. the hearing of confession by a priest), and the production of the manuals which were required to inform and support it. From a later perspective, this step, whatever its merits, set moral theology on a course which resulted in what the reforming council of the Roman Catholic church which met between 1962 and 1965 (known as Vatican II), saw as moral theology's decay.

It was the growth of the practice of confessing sins and receiving a penance along with forgiveness which lies behind the production, first of all in sixth-century Ireland but later throughout Europe, of guides to confessors, identifying and categorizing sins and the penance appropriate to them. These guides were known as "penitentials," and they sought to provide coherence, consistency, and order in a practice which was plainly liable to the variabilities of individual judgments. They represent the first step in the development of a tradition which would have its classical expression in the early eighteenth century, in the work of St. Alphonsus Liguori, later declared the patron of moral theologians, and generally deemed the greatest exponent of casuistry.

The word "casuistry" has come to be used pejoratively – it is often employed to suggest a precision and niceness in the making of distinctions which is otherwise denounced as "logic-chopping." And the later manuals of moral theology would become the stuff of ridicule for the precision with which they identified, distinguished, and categorized sin – it is doubtless false that any such manual ever informed its readers that "the sin of watching animals copulate is in proportion to the size of the animals and in inverse proportion to your distance from them" (as a distinguished professor in Cambridge joked), but as with many jokes its plausibility is the key to its being funny. There is, however, nothing wrong in thinking clearly and carefully about our moral obligations in particular and difficult cases, and thus about what constitutes wrongdoing or sin – after all, the opposite of "niceness" in moral judgments is sloppiness, and that is obviously not meritorious. Indeed, if one looks at the best examples from the tradition, the value of careful and rigorous examination of an issue is evident – thus the sixteenth-century Spanish Dominican, Vitoria, in his work *De Indiis* (On the American Indians), provides a careful and thorough demolition of the motley collection of claims which were being advanced to justify the king of Spain's conquest of the Americas.[14] Since "casuistry" means careful examination of a cause or issue or problem, there is no good reason for casuistry as such to have a bad name.

The problem lies, however, not in casuistry as such but, as Vatican II would declare, in casuistry coming to be thought of as the essence – or indeed as the extent – of moral theology or ethics. For if what is part of the subject comes to comprise the whole, much is lost. Moral theology which deals with identifying obligations and sins has cut itself off from other proper concerns and themes of Christian ethics, which will include, as in the thought of Thomas, reflection on the virtues, on God's healing grace, on the role of the church and the sacraments in sustaining and nourishing Christian faith and witness, and so on. Without these themes, a moral theology which busies itself only with identifying and categorizing sins will be prone to legalism, individualism, and moralism.

[14]   In Vitoria, *Political Writings*, ed. and trans. A. Pagden and J. Lawrance (Cambridge, 1991).

If it was the development of the practice of confession which encouraged an interest first of all in law, and thus the taking of Thomas's thought on that subject out of its wider context, it was the Reformation which would encourage the further and particular interest in discovering a law which is natural in the sense of being available to human reason apart from any theological teaching or insights. The rise of Protestantism led to the bitter religious disputes of the sixteenth and seventeenth centuries, and thus to a turn away from religion, as we shall have cause to notice, as a viable or promising source for the resolution of moral questions and conflicts. In this context ethics founded on natural law, propounded by Thomism, may seem more useful than the fully theological ethics of Thomas himself, in the very particular sense that appeal to what we might term public reasons may be grasped at as the only effective strategy for public engagement. Thomas may have ruled against polygamy because Christ had only one bride, but Catholic moralists in the period after the Reformation, being pragmatic, understandably preferred to adopt in public a style of reasoning or argument not reliant on contested religious claims. It may be perfectly reasonable to wonder, as we have, how much can actually be achieved by natural law arguments in establishing ethical claims, but it is hardly surprising that arguments of this kind had a definite appeal for Christian moralists at just those times when Christian convictions have seemed highly contested or unacceptable – and this may include our own times as much as the era of the Reformation. Thomas may not be the author of Thomism, but he is not the first or the last thinker who has been pressed into service to meet the needs of his readers.

Of course we shall have cause to wonder whether the harmony of reason and religion which Thomism presupposes, however convenient it would be, is in fact plausible. Indeed, it is not a coincidence, though it is perhaps somewhat ironic, that it is just when that supposed harmony is most doubted (as in the modern period), that it has seemed most worthwhile and urgent to insist upon it. It is in the twentieth century then, that the viability of Thomism, and the problems with it, will emerge as especially pressing questions.

4

Martin Luther: Against Ethics

In the early 1960s the Second Vatican Council lamented the sorry condition of Roman Catholic ethics, dominated as such ethics was by a Thomist approach which threatened specifically Christian themes and emphases. Some thirty years earlier, Dietrich Bonhoeffer had made a powerful complaint against the state of Protestant ethics (in his *Cost of Discipleship*, published in 1937). Bonhoeffer's protest was not aimed principally at the subject as it was taught in universities and seminaries, though it included that too; his protest was at the conception of ethics which shaped the everyday life of the Protestant churches in Germany, in which there was, to be blunt and to use his language, no struggle for holiness. The protest was prophetic. Whatever may be said of the clear-sighted heroism of certain individuals, including that of Bonhoeffer himself, hanged just before the end of the Second World War for his connections with a plot against Hitler, Christians generally, no matter what their denomination, did not prove themselves acute, courageous, or effective critics of the Nazi regime. Indeed, the truth of the matter was quite otherwise; there were plenty of Christians in Germany in the 1930s who were advocates and supporters of Nazism.

Just as the Second Vatican Council found Thomism responsible for the parlous state of Roman Catholic ethics, so Bonhoeffer chiefly blamed Lutheranism for the state of Christian life in Germany. At first sight it might seem difficult to sustain the charge against Luther. After all, there had streamed from his pen countless sermons and tracts calling his listeners and readers to observe the commandments, and to observe them not according to the letter, but according to the spirit: thus commenting on the fifth commandment ("You shall not kill"), Luther states that "'Not to kill' means not to kill either with the tongue or the hand, or with a sign or in one's heart."[1] There is, here, plainly no minimizing of the demands of the Christian life, and Luther resolutely attacked the widely accepted notion that the precepts of the Sermon on the Mount, for example, could be regarded as "counsels of perfection," addressed not to ordinary Christians, but to those, such as monks and nuns, who would excel in the religious life. The full demands of the law, the old law of the Ten Commandments, and the new law of the Gospels, fall on each and every Christian. And yet, for all that, Bonhoeffer traced to Luther's influence the poverty of Christian ethics in early twentieth-century Germany.

Bonhoeffer finds the seed of decay at the heart of Luther's message, namely in the proclamation of grace not works. With magnificent eloquence and rhetorical power, Luther condemned good works insofar as these works were understood as the means of winning salvation, whilst honoring the works in and of themselves. But, as Bonhoeffer saw it, Luther's regard for works was lost as his message was institutionalized and taken up in weekly sermons. In this context, his attack on the folly of a supposed self-righteousness founded on works was converted into a suspicion of any interest in righteousness – or in discipleship or ethics, to use less freighted terms. The result, according to Bonhoeffer, was a Christianity which was worldly and accommodating, even to the point, as it would turn out, of accommodating Hitler. As Bonhoeffer put it: "The justification of the sinner in the world became the justification of sin and the world."[2]

The misconstrual of Luther's central theme – salvation by grace not works – as a slighting of righteousness as such was the chief cause of the damage which Lutheranism did to the

[1] M. Luther, *Ten Sermons on the Catechism*, in *Luther's Works*, vol. 51 (Philadelphia, 1959), 152.
[2] D. Bonhoeffer, *Discipleship*, trans. B. Green and R. Krauss (Minneapolis, 2001), 50.

vitality of the Christian life. But two other elements in Luther's thought also contributed to the weakening of ethical thought and practice. Alongside the mistaking of Luther's attack on righteousness by works as a rejection of good works themselves, we need also to reckon with the influence of his powerful protest at the role of reason in medieval Christianity; in one of his many colorful asides, reason is "the devil's whore." Now the point of Luther's protest was at the foundational role which reason had assumed in scholastic theology, as if knowledge of God might be had by inference. But in its exuberance, and certainly when taken out of context, Luther's attack sounded very like a simple repudiation of reasoning as such – which repudiation, since Christian ethics is likely to demand careful thought about cases (or casuistry), sounds like a rejection of ethics as well.

To complete the picture, there is a third element to Luther's marginalizing of ethics, and that consists in his treatment of themes in political thought which we have touched upon as they are dealt with by Augustine and Thomas Aquinas. Luther's account of the secular, unlike Augustine's and Thomas's, seems to assign much of human life and action to a realm which is strictly outside the proper sphere of Christian interest and influence. In telling Christians to mind their own business, and in construing that business in the way he did, Luther checked and constrained Christian ethics in another highly significant way.

In defense of Luther, we need to enter a caveat which the reader may well have already anticipated. Just as Thomas is not necessarily faithfully represented in Thomism, neither is Luther by Lutheranism. The simple and stark outline of Lutheranism, to which Bonhoeffer and others objected, is something which Luther would have found objectionable too. Luther's responsibility for Lutheranism lies chiefly in the fact that his thought unfolds in response to the challenge of events, which is to say that it necessarily unfolds in a piecemeal fashion. Add to this the fact that Luther was a brilliant writer and a superb polemicist, with a particular gift for memorable one-liners, and the chances that his thought would have been appropriated whole, with the balance that might have provided, are somewhat reduced. It is only too likely that any reader will be carried away by the main lines of Luther's dramatic protestations, with all their panache and brio; altogether rather unlikely that a reader will pause, survey the whole, and carefully consider what nuances can be drawn from elsewhere in the corpus, and so correct the intense emphasis of the occasion, and thus provide for him or herself a fuller and more balanced picture. Were one to sit down and survey the whole in a scholarly fashion, there is a moral theology of great complexity and subtlety to be fathomed, and one which is not adequately represented by the three strident notes which many heard above the intended harmony of Luther's thought.[3] Be that as it may, it was these three notes which were destined to have an influence in the shaping of Protestantism in the subsequent centuries, no matter that Luther might have wished it otherwise.

The first and central element in Luther's contribution to the understanding and significance of ethics for Christian life derives from the Reformation's central proclamation of grace over works. In 1520, when Luther's disagreement with Rome was by no means beyond repair, and the Reformation certainly not yet a European movement, his message and its implications for conceptions of ethics is plain to see in a little tract, combative in tone and title, rushed off by Luther's fast-moving, eloquent, and passionate pen.

Though *The Freedom of a Christian* is only some twenty-five pages long, it contains, according to Luther, "the whole of Christian life in a brief form, provided you grasp its meaning."[4] It begins with two seemingly contradictory assertions: "A Christian is a perfectly free lord of all, subject to none. A Christian is a perfectly dutiful servant of all, subject to all."[5] Luther means to reconcile rather than oppose these claims. It is

---

[3]   On this point, see Bernd Wannenwetsch's "Luther's Moral Theology," in D. K. McKim, ed., *The Cambridge Companion to Martin Luther* (Cambridge, 2003), 120–35, and other essays in the same volume.

[4]   M. Luther, *The Freedom of a Christian*, trans. W. A. Lambert, in *Luther's Works*, vol. 31 (Philadelphia, 1957), 343.

[5]   *The Freedom of a Christian*, 344.

Bonhoeffer's point, nonetheless, that the subsequent tradition heard the first assertion rather more clearly than it heard the second, and certainly that it failed to understand the reconciliation of the two.

That Luther should place the freedom of the Christian as the first element in his account of the Christian life is a consequence of the fundamental understanding of the Gospel which had emerged from his religious struggle. As he would tell the story later, Luther had become a monk for one quite simple reason, namely to "to escape hell."[6] He had chosen the higher way, as it was thought, and had taken up the demands of poverty, chastity, and obedience and all the disciplines of the monastic life for the sake of the salvation of his soul. But in this way of life, Luther found no security. This was not because he was a bad monk, as later Counter-Reformation polemic would have it. Rather it was because the way of perfection and works contained, as he thought, a terrible contradiction – how could one achieve a perfect love of God and neighbor when the pursuit of those works was for the sake of one's own salvation? As he saw it, the religious were seeking the good of the self even in God. But how can one be selfless for the sake of the self? Once this nagging question had entered his head, he knew, even in the monastery, only a bad conscience and despair.

The way out of this despair – and hence the beginning of the Reformation – was found, in a roundabout way, as a result of a change in a university syllabus. This change was a result of a wide dissatisfaction with scholasticism – that is, with the systematic and rational presentation of theology by the "schoolmen," which had reached its apogee in the work of Aquinas but which thereafter had decayed into commentary on the commentators in ever finer detail. It was a dissatisfaction which led to a return to the study of the text of the Bible in the original languages. Luther was himself charged by his superiors with preparing lectures for new courses along these lines at

---

[6] Cited in G. Ebeling, *Luther: An Introduction to his Thought*, trans. R. A. Wilson (London, 1970), 35.

Wittenberg. Going back to the Hebrew and Greek, he worked on the Psalms and then on Paul's letters.

Now it was in Paul's letter to the Romans that Luther came upon the text which was to resolve his difficulties, or at least was to be central in his account of their resolution: "the righteous shall live by faith."[7] Reading this, he said, "I felt myself absolutely reborn, as though I had entered into the open gates of paradise itself."[8] Why? This text turned the understanding of the religious life he had learnt and lived by completely on its head. Far from believing that the righteous shall live by faith, he had learnt and lived by the view, in effect, that the faithful shall live by righteousness – that salvation depends crucially on a righteousness to be earned or achieved through the practice of good works. But the text said and taught that the righteous shall live by faith – that they are saved, not through fulfilling the commandments, but simply through faith in God. Thus righteousness is no human work at all, for we do not and cannot justify ourselves; righteousness is the unmerited gift of God to humankind in Christ, the gift by which God makes righteous, or justifies, those who have no claim to be so considered apart from his grace.

From this insight there immediately follows the heady proclamation of freedom found in Luther's little treatise of 1520: "a Christian has all that he needs in faith and needs no works to justify him; and if he has no need of works, he has no need of the law; and if he has no need of the law, surely he is free from the law."[9] Notice, the point is not that our works are inadequate, in that we cannot do enough, though that is certainly the case. It is rather that they are irrelevant to salvation, no matter how great the amount. But even more, they are worse than irrelevant; they are dangerous. Luther asserts that "faith cannot exist in connection with works – that is to say, if you at the same time claim to be justified by works, whatever their

---

[7]   Romans 1: 17.
[8]   Cited in R. Marius, *Martin Luther: The Christian Between Life and Death* (London, 1999), 193.
[9]   *The Freedom of a Christian*, 349.

character – for that would be the same as "limping with two different opinions."[10] Should a Christian "grow so foolish, however, as to presume to become righteous, free, saved and a Christian by means of some good work, he would instantly lose faith and all its benefits, a foolishness aptly illustrated in the fable of the dog who runs along a stream with a piece of meat in his mouth and, deceived by the reflection of the meat in the water, opens his mouth to snap at it and so loses both the meat and the reflection."[11] As he stresses again: "If works are sought after as a means of righteousness ... and are done under the false impression that through them one is justified, they are made necessary and freedom and faith are destroyed; and this addition to them makes them no longer good but truly damnable works. They are not free, and they blaspheme the grace of God since to justify and to save by faith belongs to the grace of God alone."[12]

So much then for the first element of Luther's paradox – "a Christian is a perfectly free lord of all, subject to none." Righteousness is a gift, not a work; and with that thought, Luther puts liberty in place of works and sweeps away the understanding of the religious and moral life which he had learnt and practiced. But what of the second element of the paradox, the part which claims that "a Christian is a perfectly dutiful servant of all"? How is it that those who may freely rely on God's grace for their justification are nonetheless in duty bound to service? Luther, preaching what he takes to be the message of St. Paul, is conscious that he, like Paul, might be accused of being antinomian (i.e., against law, *nomos* in Greek). He hastens to provide an answer. Some, he says, will "now ask: 'If faith does all things and is alone sufficient unto righteousness, why then are good works commanded? We will take our ease and do no works and be content with faith.' I answer: not so, you wicked men, not so."[13]

---

[10] *The Freedom of a Christian*, 346.
[11] *The Freedom of a Christian*, 356.
[12] *The Freedom of a Christian*, 363.
[13] *The Freedom of a Christian*, 358.

"We do not," he insists, "reject good works; on the contrary we cherish and teach them as much as possible," for, though Christians do not need works to be saved, nonetheless works are fitting for them. As Luther used to say, cows do not get to heaven by giving milk but that is what they are made for. And Christians, like cows, have their proper work, though it is not work done in pursuit of righteousness. This work is a matter of service to the welfare of the other – Christians, in Luther's audacious phrase, should be "Christs to one another."[14]

But if Christians do not do good work for the sake of salvation, why do they do it? According to Luther, this is a simple matter of the overflowing of faith. "The inner man, who by faith is created in the image of God, is both joyful and happy because of Christ in whom so many benefits are conferred upon him; and therefore it is his one occupation to serve God joyfully and without thought of gain, in love that is not constrained."[15] A Christian will think as follows, says Luther:

> Although I am an unworthy and condemned man, my God has given me in Christ all the riches of righteousness and salvation without any merit on my part, out of pure, free mercy, so that from now on I need nothing except faith which believes that this is true. Why should I not therefore freely, joyfully, with all my heart, and with an eager will do all things which I know are pleasing and acceptable to such a Father who has overwhelmed me with his inestimable riches? I will therefore give myself as a Christ to my neighbour, just as Christ offered himself to me; I will do nothing in this life except what I see is necessary, profitable and salutary to my neighbour, since through faith I have an abundance of all good things in Christ.[16]

There is no need to tell a Christian that he "ought" to do good works. "Faith teaches this work of itself." Hence, as Luther puts it elsewhere:

14   *The Freedom of a Christian*, 368.
15   *The Freedom of a Christian*, 359.
16   *The Freedom of a Christian*, 367.

It is as absurd and stupid to say: the righteous ought to do good works, as to say: God ought to do good, the sun ought to shine, the pear-tree ought to bear pears, three and seven ought to be ten; for all this follows of necessity by reason of the cause and the consequence … it all follows without commandment or bidding of any law, naturally and willingly, uncompelled and unconstrained … The sun shines by nature unbidden; the pear tree bears pears of itself, uncompelled; three and seven ought not to be ten, they are ten already. There is no need to say to our Lord God that He ought to do good, for He does it without ceasing, of Himself, willingly and with pleasure. Just so, we do not have to tell the righteous that he ought to do good works, for he does so without that, without any commandment or compulsion, because he is a new creature and a good tree.[17]

So it is that Luther claims not to discount works, but to reinstate them – even more, to reinstate them in a new and secure way. Works are liberated and enabled by true faith. In faith, I know that I need not pursue works for the sake of salvation – this is "the office and glory of grace." But in gratitude for this grace, I nonetheless devote myself to such works, genuinely directed to the welfare of others. Only thus is true goodness possible.

How then should we judge Luther's moves in this treatise, or rather the double move by which he commends Christian freedom, even while proclaiming Christians bound in service to their neighbors? We may find ourselves struggling to understand Bonhoeffer's charge that Luther has undermined the ethical life. Luther surely has a claim to have saved, rather than threatened, the ethical life, just by his radical renunciation of the perennially tempting Pelagian thought that salvation is a reward for works – the very thought which had driven Luther to the monastic life in the first place, and which, so he alleged, not only brought despair but also corrupted the moral life of the Christian. Whether within or outside a monastery, whether

[17]   Cited in P. S. Watson, *Let God be God! An Interpretation of the Theology of Martin Luther* (London, 1947), 47–8.

fasting or feeding the hungry, whether visiting the shrine of a martyr or visiting the sick, he and his contemporaries saw themselves, so he alleged, as accruing credit in an eternal bank account. They were saving up good works with the aim of accruing enough to be judged righteous. But they could never quite save enough; and in any case, this very scheme imperils ethics just as surely as crowds being issued with flags and required to wave them takes the edge off displays of patriotism. Luther's way of thought saved ethics in the sense that it allows our service of God and neighbor to be exactly that, and not a surreptitious service of self. It thus, it might be said, established the very possibility of ethical action rather than challenged it, and even as it discredited the "sacramental economy" of late medieval piety, as it has been called, it gave new recognition and honor to the simple, everyday duties of a parent, a shopkeeper, a husband, or a servant. The spiritual "heroism" of the monastery is no heroism at all, whereas the faithful fulfillment of one's everyday duties is the true demand of Christian life.

So what is the basis of Bonhoeffer's charge against Luther? It is that, in fact, the two parts of Luther's *Freedom of a Christian* were never successfully held together despite what Luther may have intended. Luther conceives of the Christian as perfectly free, the servant of none, and yet also as perfectly bound, the servant of all. But however these two parts are held together in Luther's conception of the Christian life (with the strengthening of the sense of freedom allegedly a strengthening of the very founts of gratitude which issue in service), the preaching of Luther's message resulted in what Bonhoeffer denounced as "cheap grace." This preaching took seriously the unconditional nature of God's gracious acceptance of us, but gave no clear and compelling account of the relationship between grace and discipleship now that it had abandoned the previous, as it would claim disordered, picture. That picture had made grace conditional on works, and to this the Lutheran preaching objected. But in rejecting this conditionality, and despite its intentions, the Lutheran message took shape in the popular mind, so Bonhoeffer alleges, as "the justification of sin but not of the sinner."[18] That is to say, it was a message which dealt with the symptoms of humanity's turn from God, but was unconcerned with the underlying condition. Furthermore, the Lutheran denunciation of works-righteousness rather leads to the suspicion that the very concern with righteousness constitutes rebellion against grace. And so, set on giving God's grace its due, the Christian finds no place for true discipleship. "Like ravens," says Bonhoeffer, "we have gathered around the carcass of cheap grace. From it we have imbibed the poison which has killed the following of Jesus among us."[19] So it was, observing around him as he wrote the rising and unopposed tide of Nazism, that Bonhoeffer sought to account for the particular failure of his fellow Christians – and to insist on the need for a new and better understanding of the relationship of grace and discipleship than Lutheranism had provided.

As mentioned at the outset, it was not only the vigorous preaching of grace alone which invited a turn against ethics. In the wider context of Luther's thought there were two further elements which would contribute to the same trend.

The first of these has to do with the place of reason in theology. Luther came to think that the medieval theological system which had departed so far from the message of the Bible had been misled in particular by the marriage which scholastic theology had made with philosophy, particularly Aristotelianism. Thomas, as we have seen, had sought to harmonize faith and reason, and to show that Christianity and Greek philosophy could exist in a marriage which was at once happy and fruitful. But Luther would have none of it – as he put it in one of the sharp propositions which make up his *Disputation Against Scholastic Theology* of 1517, "Aristotle is to theology as darkness is to light."[20] (In the informal version of this judgment, he was even less polite: Aristotle was the "buffoon who misled the

[18] *Discipleship*, 43
[19] *Discipleship*, 53.
[20] M. Luther, *The Disputation Against Scholastic Theology*, trans. H. J. Grimm, in *Luther's Works*, vol. 31 (Philadelphia, 1957), proposition 50.

Church.") Luther saw no happy marriage here, but rather the subjection of Christianity to an essentially incompatible partner, depriving Christianity of its authentic character and insights. It was this subjection which rendered late medieval Christianity thoroughly Pelagian: one aspect of that Pelagianism we have already touched upon, the moral Pelagianism which understood the Christian life as a work seeking grace as its reward. But Luther also discerned what one might term an intellectual or epistemological Pelagianism: just as in the popular piety to which he objected we are supposed to be able to do God's will by our own unassisted efforts, so also, according to the scholastics, we could know at least something of God's will by the exercise of our reason. In that same *Disputation*, Luther dismisses both elements at once: "man by nature has neither correct precept nor good will"[21] – that is, man, without grace, is not only unable to will the good, but unable even to know it.

An interest in ethics becomes presumptuous in the Lutheran scheme as suggesting reliance on works and not on grace alone; but when we add in the suspicion of reason as indicating human pride, the ethicist threatens to compound his or her sin, especially in the practice of casuistry. Casuistry means no more than reasoning about cases – and even the thinker who eschews any role for reason in determining the principles which are the basis for ethical thought will have to deploy reason in considering the application of these principles. In that sense, Luther is as much a casuist as those he denounces – his treatments of questions about marriage and usury prove the point. Luther was not against reason and logic, but in fact only against the thought that one might be saved by a syllogism. But no matter that he intended no blanket dismissal of reason, his barbed slurs against reason, along with the lauding of grace, further the sense that ethics is an "inherently doubtful enterprise."[22]

There is, however, a third and extremely significant element to add to the picture, and this relates to Luther's treatment of

[21]   *Disputation Against Scholastic Theology*, proposition 17.
[22]   To use Stanley Hauerwas's characterization of the Protestant suspicion of ethics; see *The Peaceable Kingdom* (London, 1984), 52.

the secular realm. As we have seen, Augustine conceived of human society by means of a contrast between "two cities," earthly and heavenly. But these two cities, very importantly, occupy the same space, so to speak. They are related not spatially, but temporally or eschatologically – which is to say that the "secular" or the "worldly" represents an epoch in which the heavenly city is being revealed, not an autonomous realm marked out by a boundary. The worldly is definitely not set to one side in this way of thinking, but always remains within the one sphere of theological concern and interest. Luther, in dealing with a particular and practical problem, transposed the Augustinian scheme by converting the relationship of the two cities into a quite different one, based on a functional division of the worldly and the spiritual.

Less than two years after he had written *The Freedom of a Christian*, Luther published his translation of the New Testament. In November 1522 one of the German princes issued an edict prohibiting its sale and requiring the surrender of any copies already in private hands. Thus Luther was spurred on by this incident to set out his thought on the rights, duties, and limits of secular rule, and in so doing marked out boundaries between the spiritual and the secular realms based on difference of role or function.

What he wrote in *On Secular Authority*[23] was written to save his New Testament from the hands of ungodly princes; bibles were not the business of princes, and if they sought to confiscate them, they were to be resisted. But the move which gave the spiritual realm to the church, and kept princes at bay in that regard, by the same token gave the secular to the state and told the church to mind its own business, which is precisely spiritual and not worldly. It was this Lutheran sense of a division of roles, along with both the mishandling of the relationship between grace and discipleship, and furthermore the very suspicion of ethical reasoning, which helps to explain the extraordinary quiescence of the Protestant churches in Germany not

---

[23]   M. Luther, *On Secular Authority*, in *Luther and Calvin on Secular Authority*, ed. and trans. H. Höpfl (Cambridge, 1991).

just in the early, but also in the later, years of the 1930s. The freedom of the church to order its own affairs was defended with a certain vigor; thus the right to ordain Jews was a cause to which many could rally. But that the church might have a critical responsibility in relation to the wider society, and thus a duty to protest at the proscription and persecution of Jews: this was a thought which Luther's immediate solution to the problem of the confiscation of bibles did much to discourage.

Luther's *Freedom of a Christian* is a powerful and important book, providing a trenchant critique of what is a very common and tempting understanding of the Christian life as a matter of works done for the sake of a reward. Luther is right that the Christian life is not to be thought of as a sort of demanding fitness regime, at the end of which we might make the grade and win an entry ticket to heaven. Instead, he insists that the Christian life is one of liberty – the liberty which comes from knowing that one is justified by God's grace, and so may therefore use one's life wholly and freely, not to secure one's own salvation, but rather to address the needs of others.

But when Luther says that this book contains "the whole of the Christian life," he surely rather overstates the case, and is in danger of leaving us, as Bonhoeffer's charge suggests, with what can only be the beginning of the matter, but not its end and entire content. Luther was right in identifying and criticizing the temptation, which one might detect even in the *Rule of St Benedict* and which Luther certainly found in the piety of the late Middle Ages, of construing the Christian life as a matter of work and reward. That we cannot make ourselves righteous before God by works, but that God himself makes us righteous in Christ, is certainly a message of liberation which opens up the possibility of genuinely other-regarding action. But the announcement of our liberation surely invites us to ask, "liberation for what?" Here Luther rather fails us. His denunciation of works casts a suspicion over the very subject of ethics as a hankering after righteousness through our own efforts and discourages, as Bonhoeffer says, the attempt to articulate the meaning of discipleship. And his animadversions against reason seem further to discourage this articulation, by denying the propriety of that careful and patient reflection on cases which must surely constitute a part of what is involved in critical engagement with the problems and questions life throws up. And, if this is not enough, his seeming grant of autonomy to the secular realm drastically limits the scope of Christian ethics, since what might been thought to have belonged to its territory is ruled out of bounds.

As we said at the outset, Luther might well protest that these three elements do not fairly represent his thought. If that is so, he would have cause to regret the influence of Lutheranism as much as did its later critics, especially for ethics; for whereas its message has been summed up in the assertion that "morality is found beyond the law," it rather looks as if morality was lost, not found, beyond the law.

5

Butler, Kant, and Kierkegaard: The Turn to the Subject

Not all contributions to Christian thought and doctrine have obvious or immediate significance, but plainly Luther's did. To put it pejoratively, Luther divided the church. And this fact alone, apart from any specific and direct contribution to the understanding of morals and morality, would have implications for Christian ethics. Perhaps nothing is quite so effective in suggesting that something is questionable than its being questioned, and the division between Christians on all sorts of matters, including ethical matters, drew attention to the questionable nature of claims and counter-claims in this sphere. That the disagreements were conducted not only in sharp words, but, in the century following Luther's death, in some very sharp exchanges of blows, served all the more to draw attention to the potential for dispute.

It would be a mistake, however, to think of the Reformation, and the manifestation of divisions within Christianity which Luther precipitated, as other than the proximate cause of the crisis of justification for ethics which emerged in the late seventeenth century. This crisis was a symptom of other and broader trends of which the Reformation itself was an expression. Luther's repudiation of scholasticism, which was a decisive moment in his intellectual journey, was a repudiation partly constitutive of the grandly named Renaissance, which in turn led on to the even more grandly named Enlightenment. What lay at the basis of the Renaissance was the rediscovery, from classical civilization, of the power of human thought, a power which would be further deployed in the Enlightenment, where reason becomes the watchword.

But the affirmation of the power of reason is also an assertion of its limits. If reason is the basis for approaching and
understanding the world, and one which provides ground for a
certain intellectual confidence, reason has its scope or bounds.
And the question as to whether moral judgments lie within or
beyond the scope of reason is one which would have been
posed, whether or not the disputes surrounding religious belief
and practice associated with the Reformation had drawn attention to the sharp disagreements within this domain.

Michel de Montaigne (1533–92), living in and around
Bordeaux during the period of political instability in France
which was fueled by contention between Catholics and the
Huguenots (as the French Protestants were known), had first-
hand experience of these sharp disagreements. So, commenting
on the stories of cannibalism which were regularly brought
back from the then still newly discovered "New World," he
rather understandably turns to matters closer to home:

> I am not so much concerned that we should remark on the hor-
> rible barbarity of such acts, as that, whilst rightly judging their
> errors, we should be so blind to our own. I think that there is
> more barbarity in eating a live than a dead man, in tearing on
> the rack and torturing the body of man still full of feeling, in
> roasting him piecemeal and giving him to be bitten and mangled
> by dogs and swine (as we have not only read, but seen within
> fresh memory, not between old enemies, but between neighbours
> and fellow citizens, and, what is worse, under the cloak of piety
> and religion), than in roasting and eating him after he is dead.[1]

In response to religious contention of the kind to which
Montaigne refers, one might, of course, be led to a simple and
pragmatic rejection of conviction. If conviction leads to barbar-
ity, better to do without conviction. But in Montaigne this
rejection has a theoretical underpinning. It draws on a skeptical
tradition which was as much a part of the inheritance from the
classical world as the affirmation of reason's power.

[1]   M. de Montaigne, *Essays*, trans. E. J. Trechmann (London, 1935), vol. 1,
essay xxxi, 209–10.

"What kind of truth," Montaigne famously asks, "can be limited by a range of mountains, becoming a lie for the world on the other side?"[2] Our convictions, he means to say, are very much *our* convictions. Contention surrounding such convictions is the outward and visible sign of the truth that we don't have the means decisively to support and justify them. So if customs and customary beliefs are to be respected, as Montaigne says they are, they are respected simply as customs and beliefs, and not as truths. This is indeed, according to Montaigne, a recipe for civil and religious peace; but Montaigne is a skeptic by conviction, so to speak, as much as by policy.

Another victim of the political instability of the century which followed Luther's death, Thomas Hobbes (1588–1679), was also a skeptic, but of an altogether more robust kind. Montaigne, it is true, ended up on the Index,[3] but he was no outspoken revolutionary. His heirs in the next generation were less retiring, and Hobbes would serve as a bête noire for moralists, Christian and otherwise, for much of the eighteenth century; he converted the gentle and unsystematic questioning of Montaigne into an altogether more doctrinaire skepticism which included a commitment to materialism, psychological hedonism (the belief that humans always act for the sake of pleasure), and, arguably, a denial of free will.

But what chiefly concerns us is his questioning of morals and his insistence that the "words good, evil and contemptible, are ever used with relation to the person that useth them, there being nothing simply and absolutely so, nor any common rule of good or evil, to be taken from the nature of objects themselves."[4] The word "relativism" was to be coined a lot later, in the nineteenth century in fact; but we have an instance of it here, long before it was named. Moral judgments says Hobbes, are in relation "to the person that useth them."

---

[2]   *An Apology for Raymond Sebond*, trans. M. A. Screech (London, 1987), 160.
[3]   i.e. the list of prohibited books first issued by the Inquisition in the sixteenth century.
[4]   T. Hobbes, *Leviathan*, Book 1, ch. 6; in many editions.

It was this particular challenge, so sharply posed by Hobbes, which was the immediate provocation to many to provide a clear justification of ethical judgment. And perhaps no such justification is quite as clear and simple as the one advanced by Joseph Butler (1692–1752), sometime bishop of Bristol. Immanuel Kant (1724–1804) sympathized with the project of justification, but not with Butler's attempted solution to it, and advanced a highly influential alternative. Søren Kierkegaard (1813–55) was in turn dissatisfied with Kant's approach, specifically from a Christian viewpoint.

In the company of these three, then, we shall make our way (rather rapidly it must be admitted), from the sixteenth to the mid-nineteenth century, noting at the outset that, for all their differences, they have one important thing in common. In responding to the crisis of justification, they turn to the moral subject. Eschewing an appeal to authority or to an external law (either the written law of Scripture or the natural law available to reason), they each, albeit in different ways, look to the subject and to the subject's inwardness for morality's vindication.

The inwardness to which Butler appeals he calls "conscience," and his argument has the brevity and simplicity of many vindications of morality. Specifically arguing against Hobbes's relativism, Butler is clear and straightforward. When we reflect on our actions and characters, Butler contends, "we naturally and unavoidably approve some actions, under the peculiar view of their being virtuous and of good desert, and disapprove others as vicious and of ill desert."[5] That we have "this moral approving and disproving faculty is certain," he insists, "from our experiencing it in ourselves and recognizing it in each other."[6] We and others judge this or that right or wrong. Our language and behavior are, he says,

> formed upon supposition of such a moral faculty, whether called
> conscience, moral reason, moral sense, or divine reason; whether

[5] J. Butler, "A Dissertation Upon the Nature of Virtue," section 1; first published as an appendix to Book 1, ch. 3, of Butler's *Analogy of Religion* of 1736, but regularly published separately, especially with Butler's sermons.
[6] Ibid.

considered as a sentiment of the understanding or as a perception of the heart, or, which seems the truth, as including both.
Nor is it at all doubtful in the general what course of action this
faculty, or practical discerning power within us, approves and
what it disapproves. For, as much as it has been disputed wherein
virtue consists, or whatever ground for doubt there may be
about particulars, yet, in general, there is in reality an universally acknowledged standard of it. It is that which all ages and
all countries have made profession of in public; it is that which
every man you meet puts on the show of; it is that which the
primary and fundamental laws of all civil constitutions over the
face of the earth make it their business and endeavour to enforce
the practice of upon mankind, namely justice, veracity and
regard to common good.[7]

Now Butler, we should remind ourselves, was no fool.
In particular, his critique of Hobbes's psychological hedonism
is, as subsequent commentators (including the great David
Hume, generally no friend to bishops) have generally agreed,
subtle and broadly persuasive. In comparison, Hobbes's theory
of human motivation, which has us all, always, acting for the
sake of pleasure, seems simplistic and flat. But the modern
reader is inclined to treat Butler as a fool of the first order in
making an argument on behalf of morality by appealing to conscience and moral judgment. Surely, the modern reader is
inclined to think, appeal to private judgment will only work as
a vindication of morality just so far as this private judgment is,
as it turns out, a shared, social judgment (as Butler presupposes). But it is not. There are, for example, cannibals. And
since it is not the case that there is the shared, social judgment
his argument needs, Butler turns out to be a fool (albeit one
who wrote quite well).

This will not do, however, for a number of reasons. Apart
from anything else, Butler would have known about cannibals –
if only from reading *Robinson Crusoe* and not from any
personal acquaintance gained in the course of fulfilling his

[7] Ibid.

ecclesiastical duties. It seems highly unlikely, then, that his argument on behalf of the authority of conscience as a universal faculty of moral judgment comes crashing down because of the blindingly obvious fact of moral disagreement. Instead, whilst Butler does indeed believe that there is general agreement in moral belief and practice in virtue of the workings of conscience, he can nonetheless admit the existence of particular disagreements and offer explanations of them, compatible with his general approach.

There are two fairly obvious moves which Butler could make. First, he can simply argue that the cannibals (to stick with them), are in bad faith. They have bad consciences, that is to say, and if so, presumably don't enjoy their meals as much as they might, and even perhaps lie awake with a sort of moral indigestion. Alternatively, the objectivist might argue that if this is not so (and cannibals in fact sleep very soundly at night), it is simply because the cannibals have not, as yet, exercised their consciences. It is no objection to a theory of the kind Butler espouses that, for example, children do not concur in adults' moral judgments. All that is required for Butler to claim is that when they come to their moral senses and exercise a mature judgment, they will concur. So with the cannibals. Of course, it is very unlikely that any real cannibals are much like small infants in general – after all, they probably regulate their affairs in sophisticated ways, relying, perhaps, on all sorts of developed moral notions, including, for example, notions of duty, justice, and fairness. But if so, Butler can claim that they have simply not applied their conscience to the subject in hand.

The point here is not to advance or commend Butler's argument, but simply to note that the fact of moral disagreements, radical or otherwise, would come as no surprise to him, and his moral theory is not resourceless when it encounters such disagreements. And the arguments which we have imagined might be made on his behalf are open to confirmation or refutation in the light of empirical evidence of various kinds. We can, in principle, discover that the cannibals really do have bad consciences, or that they modify their diets as they encounter our objections, or whatever it might be. Moral disagreements, however widespread and deep they seem, may not be real disagreements, or where they are, may be resolved by resort to reasons and considerations of various kinds.

It is interesting to note, of course, that Butler's chief critics do not, as seems natural to many modern readers, challenge the existence of the broad moral consensus on which his theory depends. Notice then, for example, that Hume's disagreement with Butler does not rest on a rejection of Butler's belief in a general consensus in moral approbation – what we might term the "intersubjectivity" of the individual judgments of individual subjects. What he does dispute is Butler's explanation of that intersubjectivity. That is to say, Hume's famed moral skepticism is not a skepticism about what constitutes virtue or vice in general, and is certainly not founded on the supposed fact of widespread disagreements in practice. Hume supposes that virtue very plainly consists in the possession of the sort of character and virtues Jane Austen gives to her heroes, possessed as they are of honesty, modesty, magnanimity, proper pride, and the like. He shows no sign of thinking that there is any serious disagreement about this; nor does the skeptical Scot wish us to repudiate, or even to doubt, the authority of morals and moral judgment. His skepticism is directed specifically at Butler's explanation of this consensus by reference to a moral faculty of understanding. This is "metaphysics" and an "abstruse hypothesis"; by contrast, "The hypothesis which we embrace is plain. It maintains that morality is determined by sentiment."[8] It is feeling, not thinking, which ensures agreement. But morality, a common morality, is indeed determined by those sentiments which belong to human nature – and is none the worse for that.

If Hume thought that Butler's justification of moral judgment said too much (and could be naturalized, so to speak, by reference to sentiments rather than faculties of judgment), Kant thought it said too little. Again, there is no questioning of the commonality of moral judgment – Kant does not bring forward cannibals or any others to challenge what Butler takes to be the

[8]   D. Hume, *An Enquiry Concerning the Principles of Morals*, in *Enquiries*, ed. L. A. Selby-Bigge, 3rd edn. (Oxford, 1975), 289.

deliveries of conscience. Like Butler, he thinks that what is morally required of us is generally and commonly known. His objection is rather that Butler's is not really a theory of moral obligation at all. As he puts it, "universality of assent does not prove the objective validity of a judgment (i.e., its validity as cognition)."[9] That is to say that even where there is, as supposed, universal agreement, this agreement would be, for all we know, subjective, and contingent – on our desiring the same ends, having the same sentiments, obeying the same god, or whatever. Agreement does not prove objectivity, but rather "only objective validity constitutes the ground of a necessary universal agreement."[10] And "objective necessity" is "to be found only in *a priori* judgments"[11] – that is, in the judgment of reason. "Pure philosophy ... must come first, and without it there can be no moral philosophy at all."[12] It is not that Butler's argument fails, but rather that, even if it succeeds, it is insufficient to provide a genuine justification of moral obligation.

According to Kant's analysis, moral obligation is absolute – to use his term, it expresses a "categorical imperative." An imperative ("do this," "do that"), is hypothetical insofar as it identifies a means to some end where the end is, so to speak, optional – "give up smoking" is a hypothetical command in the very sense that it presupposes, as a hypothesis, my wanting to avoid various diseases; "take some exercise" presupposes my not wanting to get fat. If I am told to do either, I might protest that I do not mind getting ill or fat, or whatever. By contrast, "a categorical imperative would be one which represented an action as objectively necessary in itself apart from its relation to a further end."[13] "Keep your promises," "do not lie," "stop torturing me" – these imperatives seem categorical just in the

[9]   I. Kant, *Critique of Practical Reason*, trans. and ed. M. Gregor (Cambridge, 1997), 10.
[10]   Ibid.
[11]   Ibid.
[12]   I. Kant, *Groundwork of the Metaphysic of Morals*, trans. H. J. Paton as *The Moral Law* (London, 1948), 57.
[13]   *Groundwork of the Metaphysic of Morals*, 78.

sense that they don't presuppose some end, which you may or may not share, and lacking which excuses you from obeying them. And according to Kant, it is being categorical which is characteristic of moral obligations, which bind us regardless of our ends and inclinations. We know ourselves as bound and it is in the nature of such obligation that it requires obedience of us categorically, regardless of inclination.

What Kant's moral philosophy provides is an analysis of moral obligation so understood; that there is such an obligation, that we are obliged by the "moral law within,"[14] is not so much a conclusion for which Kant argues, but rather a premise from which he begins. The content of his moral philosophy is thus not devoted to the justification or vindication of such an obligation, but to our understanding of it. What, in other words, must be true given that we are subject to such imperatives? And how are we to conceive of the general form or character of the moral law? That there are indeed such categorical imperatives is not, however, established, but rather assumed.

The intellectual pyrotechnics with which Kant accomplishes his project are, without question, worthy of awe. Kant argues that for there to be obligations of this kind, they must oblige rational agents simply as a rational agents. That is to say, if a rational agent is bound by an interest, he or she is bound hypothetically. But to be bound as such, and hence categorically, is to be bound by one's own willing of the moral law as a law of reason. Only as willing his or her own law as a reasonable and autonomous subject can an agent be subject to such an imperative. But to think of oneself as an autonomous moral agent is to think of oneself as free. Thus, from the existence of moral duty we are led to postulate free will, at least as a "regulative ideal" – and further, according to arguments of even greater ambition, abstractness, and (it must be added) contentiousness, to postulate immortality and God.

The nature and import, let alone the success, of Kant's arguments to these conclusions are vexed questions. But even

---

[14]   Kant, *Critique of Practical Reason*, 133.

without pursuing those questions, one may wonder whether the results which are promised, even supposing they are achieved, are really worth the effort – at least in relation to what we have referred to as the crisis of justification epitomized in the blatant skepticism of Hobbes. Butler and Hume, as we noted, were setting out to answer Hobbes (or the more gentle skepticism of Montaigne). Hume thought that Butler had too much metaphysics, and that morality could be vindicated quite modestly as the expression of natural human sentiments. Kant's complaint against both was not that their answers were unsuccessful as such, but rather that they did not go far enough, and he provides what he takes to be a more adequate account of the logic and presuppositions of moral obligation. But just insofar as this account depends on our consciousness of "the moral law within," to use again Kant's well-known expression, it is not clear how far we have advanced, other than conceptually, beyond the simple and homely conscience to which Butler appealed. The Kantian subject is more self-conscious than the Butlerian subject, and provides a more thorough and philosophically articulate analysis of what his or her subjectivity presupposes. But still it seems to be the subject and the subject's consciousness to which Kant appeals.

Kierkegaard found human relationships rather difficult, but even from a simple intellectual standpoint he would have been a friend to neither Butler nor Kant. Both he would regard as propounding understandings of moral obligation inimical to Christianity, properly understood, and it is in this way that he serves to take our story forwards. Butler and Kant were both influential figures, and provided a settlement of the question of justification raised so sharply by Hobbes which would serve to shape much of both Christian and secular ethics in the nineteenth century. At his death in mid-century, Kierkegaard was, by contrast, very definitely a dormant force. His works arise from an intensity of concern and concentration which makes few concessions to the reader; his intention in individual works is sometimes concealed and the relationship of one to another, a matter of some complexity; furthermore, though he can hardly be criticized very harshly on this count, he wrote in Danish.

None of this served to speed the reception of his ideas. But some fifty years after his death, at the beginning of the twentieth century, his voice was heard and reckoned with, and as it concerns us, made one very telling point. And that is, in effect, that the moral consensus constructed in the eighteenth century, whatever else might be said for or against it, was not an explication, but a betrayal, of Christianity.

Kierkegaard's little book *Fear and Trembling* has a form and logic which resemble the form and logic of Kant's enquiries. Kant asks the following question: what is presupposed philosophically, by our being morally obliged? Kierkegaard asks a parallel question in *Fear and Trembling*, but one which aims, in effect, to challenge the adequacy of Kant's answer from the point of view of faith. The question is: what is presupposed philosophically and religiously, including in relation to ethics, by faith in God? Abraham is the Bible's great exemplar of faith, and the epitome of Abraham's faith is found in his readiness to obey God's command to him to sacrifice his son, Isaac. According to Kierkegaard, the exploration of the presuppositions involved in holding such faith to be praiseworthy demonstrates the sheer inadequacy of Kant's conception of ethics for Christianity properly conceived.

Abraham presents no challenge to the worldly Protestantism in which Kierkegaard had grown up and which he despised, just because Abraham's story is either not understood or is simply discounted:

> We glorify Abraham, but how? We recite the whole story in clichés: "The great thing was that he loved God in such a way that he was willing to offer him the best." That is very true, but "the best" is a vague term. Mentally and orally we homologise Isaac and the best, and the contemplator can very well smoke his pipe while cogitating, and the listener may well stretch out his legs comfortably. ... So we talk and in the process of talking interchange the two terms, Isaac and the best, and everything goes fine.[15]

---

[15]   S. Kierkegaard, *Fear and Trembling*, trans. H. V. Hong and E. H. Hong (Princeton, 1983), 28.

The interchange is, however, illegitimate. It gives us a "cheap edition of Abraham."[16] But Abraham does not give of his best – "The ethical expression for what Abraham did is that he meant to murder Isaac; the religious expression is that he meant to sacrifice Isaac."[17]

Once we have dispensed with the "cheap edition," we can only speak of this Abraham, the real Abraham, with the "fear and trembling" of Kierkegaard's title. What we cannot do is to understand Abraham within the ethical as Kant, and later Hegel, understood it. Why not? Kierkegaard's dense formulation of the point is this:

> The ethical is as such the universal, and as the universal it applies to everyone, which from another angle means that it applies at all times. It rests immanent in itself, has nothing outside itself which is its telos, but is itself the telos for everything outside itself. The single individual ... has his telos in the universal, and it is his ethical task continually to express himself in this, to annul his singularity in order to become the universal.... [But] faith is precisely the paradox that the single individual as the single individual is higher than the universal, is justified before it, not as inferior to it but as superior ... that the single individual as the single individual stands in an absolute relation to the absolute. This position cannot be mediated ...[18]

The formulation is dense, but the central point is clear enough. According to many understandings of ethics (including the understanding advanced by Kant), our individual duties or obligations arise from universally binding rules of conduct which command an act as good in itself and therefore as necessary for a will which is to conform to reason. This is what Kant means by categorical imperatives. The ethical is universal and is "immanent in itself" – that is to say, it is not warranted by anything outside itself, but is itself the end in terms of which all else must be measured.

[16]   *Fear and Trembling*, 53.
[17]   *Fear and Trembling*, 30.
[18]   *Fear and Trembling*, 54–6.

But the story of Abraham cannot be understood in these terms. Far from being understood from within the ethical, "the story of Abraham contains … a teleological suspension of the ethical." Abraham, note, is not a tragic hero – "Abraham does not have the middle term that saves the tragic hero."[19] In other words, Abraham is not one of those figures who, finding themselves tragically caught in a conflict between two duties, heroically resolves this conflict in favor of the higher duty – so it was with Brutus, who had his sons executed for their rebellion against the state, on the basis that he had a higher duty to the state than to his sons. Thus "the tragic hero is still within the ethical. … Here there can be no question of a teleological suspension of the ethical itself."[20] But Abraham's "situation is different. By his act he transgressed the ethical altogether and had a higher telos outside it, in relation to which he suspended it."[21] Far from being of any use in explaining what he did, "the ethical in the sense of the moral is entirely beside the point."[22] Indeed, in relation to Abraham's task, that of proving his faith in God, "the temptation is the ethical itself"[23] – that is to say, it stands between him and his doing what he should do. If he is to do it, he will do it in virtue of his faith, in which "the single individual [has become] higher than the universal."

> This is the paradox, which cannot be mediated. How he entered into it is just as inexplicable as how he remains in it. If this is not Abraham's situation, then Abraham is not even a tragic hero but a murderer.[24]

Either the "single individual is higher than the universal and as the single individual stands in an absolute relation to the absolute – … or else Abraham is lost."[25]

---

[19]   *Fear and Trembling*, 57.
[20]   *Fear and Trembling*, 59.
[21]   Ibid.
[22]   Ibid.
[23]   *Fear and Trembling*, 60.
[24]   *Fear and Trembling*, 66.
[25]   *Fear and Trembling*, 81.

This, however, is just what Kantian ethics cannot allow, the possibility of this relationship of the individual to the absolute. If there is to be this relationship, and a teleological suspension of the ethical, then there must be something – the religious – which stands higher than the ethical. But as Kant famously asserted, "Even the Holy One of the gospel must first be compared with our ideal of moral perfection, before we can recognise him to be such."[26] Hence, discussing the story which Kierkegaard seeks to elucidate, Kant asserts that Abraham should have replied to the so-called divine command as follows: "That I ought not to kill my good son is quite certain. But that you, this apparition, are God – of that I am not certain, and never can be, even if this voice rings down to me from ... heaven."[27] Kant corrects Abraham; Kierkegaard tries to make sense of him.

We have followed a somewhat curious path in this chapter. In response to the skeptical challenge so sharply posed by Hobbes, the turn to the subject seemed a promising strategy. In their very different ways, Butler, Hume, and Kant (the latter outbidding the other two), seemed to find in the human subject a basis for a vindication of morality. Kierkegaard's appeal to a yet more radical subjectivity challenges this consensus on behalf of what he would see as authentic Christianity. According to Kierkegaard, the defense of ethics which is offered by Butler, Hume, and Kant, however it works in general, is problematic for Christianity. In other words, whether or not the strategy taken against the skeptics works for morality in general, Kierkegaard protests that it does not serve Christianity. Plausibility for ethics has been bought at the cost of the loss of the sharp challenge to the world which is essential to true Christianity.

Kant's account of practical reason, and his vindication of the moral law within, was the second part of his vast and breathtakingly ambitious philosophical project. The first part had

[26]   *Groundwork of the Metaphysic of Morals*, 73.
[27]   I. Kant, *Conflict of the Faculties*, trans. M. Gregor, in *Religion and Rational Theology: The Cambridge Edition of the Works of Immanuel Kant* (Cambridge, 1996), 283.

been in the critique of pure reason – "critique" in the sense of setting its bounds and limits. Beyond these bounds, in an afterthought to his central concerns, he had placed religious metaphysics. And he sought to show not that certain arguments for the existence of God did not work, but, far more sweepingly, that no such argument could work. He had attacked reason, he said, to make way for faith.

His legacy to nineteenth-century Christianity was profound and complex, but at its core lay Kant's inversion of the normal relationship between ethics and metaphysics. To put it informally, ethics was not to be derived from belief in God, but rather claims about God were to be understood as expressions of ethics. And in his *Religion Within the Bounds of Reason Alone*, Kant offered a reading of Christian doctrine as, in essence, stories expressing moral truths. As the cords of religious skepticism – philosophical, scientific, and historical – were bound tighter and tighter in the nineteenth century, Christianity came more and more to adopt a similar self-understanding, at least implicitly, in its emphasis on the sureness of morality, and in its increasing uncertainty in relation to the ground and justification of its doctrines.

Kierkegaard's protest against such an understanding of Christianity would sound again, but through the nineteenth century it lay neglected and unheard. When it did emerge, the problem of ethics would look quite different. By then, the turn to the subject which had grown out of the Enlightenment had faced questioning of a new and pressing kind, and what had seemed a promising strategy in response to Hobbes would now seem the last gasp of the vague anthropological optimism which was a legacy of the Renaissance.

6

Nietzsche and the Genealogists: Suspecting the Subject

As we saw in the previous chapter, the problem of moral relativism as it was posed in the early and mid-seventeenth century drew from a range of eighteenth-century thinkers a response which involved a turn to the subject. In search of moral authority, moralists (Christian and otherwise), turned not outwards to the world or to the will of God, but inwards to the "moral law within," to the moral sense of right and wrong, to conscience, to the stirrings of the heart, to an inner light, or to natural human sentiments. The rule of right was to be found in the subject, not outside. And consensus in moral judgments (if not on moral theory), was the token of this inner truth.

The human subject entered the nineteenth century, then, as a moral being, but by the end of that same century the subject's character would be darkened immeasurably. The great fathers of suspicion, Marx, Darwin, and Nietzsche (and their twentieth-century colleague Freud), saw the human subject in a different light. It was not, let us notice, that they doubted the honesty of the human subject who conceived of him or herself in the idealizing terms of the eighteenth century. The noble Kantian with his or her severe and unwavering regard for duty was no simple liar. It was rather that beneath his or her immediate thoughts and motivations there lurked deeper forces than appeared on the surface, impenetrable to mere self-consciousness or momentary reflection. As to what these forces were, there was no ready agreement – but that such forces lay underneath the surface was now to be taken for granted. After these thinkers, consciousness – moral or otherwise – would always be open to the question of whether or not it was false consciousness. Thus the self which emerges in the twentieth century is altogether more doubtful than the self we left at the end of the eighteenth, and doubtful not only of itself, but of other selves too – or perhaps especially of other selves. This disenchantment of the self would make the turn to the subject seem no longer promising as a solution to the problem of ethics, but in fact quite hopeless. Insofar as Christianity had invested in such strategies (as English and German Protestantism had), it had made a decidedly dubious investment.

As I have noted already, the various genealogists are, in a sense, at odds one with another in offering alternatives to the eighteenth-century faith in the moral subject. Each has a different suspicion of the simple explanation of moral judgment, and agreement in moral judgment, by reference to moral truth. Marx rejects the "eternal truths" of religion and morality as, in fact, determined by, and expressive of, class interests[1] – and thus, in contrast to Nietzsche's account, for Marx morality is not the means by which the weak revenge themselves on the strong, but the means by which the strong oppress the weak. Darwin, on the other hand, proposes, in *The Descent of Man*, to approach the moral sense or conscience "from the side of natural history," attempting "to see how far the study of the lower animals can throw light on the highest psychical faculties of man";[2] the light it throws, so he contends, is just that the origins of these faculties can be traced to natural and adaptive features of animal life. Freud offers a different naturalism, finding the origin of morality's commands to duty and selflessness not in the Kantian subject as bound by reason, but in the superego shaped by the demands of parents and society. Thus the genealogists are certainly not united in the genealogy they advance. But this is, in itself, of far less interest than the promise of their common project to tender natural, causal explanations for morality – explanations which either positively eschew, or at least have no obvious need for, references to truth.

[1]   In, for example, *The Communist Manifesto* (in very many editions).
[2]   C. Darwin, *The Descent of Man* (London, 1871), 71.

Nietzsche's *On the Genealogy of Morals* lies close to our concerns, and is crucial in advancing the relativist case beyond what one might think of as the bald assertions of Hobbes. Hobbes, as we have seen, claimed that moral judgments are in "relation to the person that useth them"; that is, that judgments of good and bad, right and wrong, are not to be explained by reference to an object of judgment which would make them true or false, but by the subject making the judgment. But then the question arises, why do people make these judgments, and broadly seem to agree on them, if there really is no truth at stake here? If, according to relativism, moral judgments are in some sense erroneous, we need an explanation not only of the widespread error, but also and more importantly of agreement in error – of the intersubjectivity on which many defenders of ethics had relied. Without that explanation, the relativist case seems more asserted than argued.

It is this element in the relativist critique of morals which *On the Genealogy of Morals* attempts to supply, as the title suggests. Nietzsche proffers an alternative account of the genesis of morality from the one which rests on the simple thought that morality expresses truth. Far from expressing some constant and enduring insight, Nietzsche claims, morality (meaning specifically morality as it has been understood in the Western, Christian tradition), arises from feelings of "ressentiment" – he uses the French word to describe the experience from which the birth of values stems, finding no German word for it; but the English "resentment" will serve, so long as we keep in mind the particular attitude to which Nietzsche refers and the wider psychological phenomenon of which it is constitutive. Morality – or "slave morality" as he terms it – begins "when ressentiment itself turns creative and gives birth to values."[3] From this original moment, guilt, bad conscience, and asceticism arise, and with them the "tragedy" of morality.

According to Nietzsche, resentment occurs when a wrong, or at least a perceived wrong, is suffered by those who, "being

---

[3]   F. Nietzsche, *On the Genealogy of Morals*, trans. C. Diethe (Cambridge, 1994), I. 10; reference throughout is to essay number and section.

denied the proper response of action, compensate for it only with imaginary revenge."[4] The strong deal with wrongs by action aimed at redressing them. And, being strong, they are unlikely to notice wrongs or slights which hardly touch them. Similarly, and for the reason that they have an outlet in action, they are unlikely to experience those feelings of envy and jealousy to which the impotent are especially prone. In the first place they are not inclined to make the comparisons which are fundamental to jealousy or envy. And in any case, the desire for something possessed by another will, in the case of the strong, typically find expression in action to obtain it. With the weak it is quite different. Wrongs must be borne rather than redressed, and for that reason will be strongly felt. Furthermore wrongs will be expected, and in this state of anticipation, will be experienced even where no wrong was intended. Those who are responsible for these real or imagined wrongs will, of course, be resented; and since they can be neither punished nor emulated, desire for what they are and have will issue not in action, but simply in envy of their power, position, and possessions.

Now this is where resentment turns creative. For the envy or jealousy which expresses a vain desire for what others have will also foster and nurture the sense of grievance which the victims of real or imagined wrongs have towards the great. Led by these feelings, the weak will come to blame these others for what they themselves lack. And even the weak, or especially the weak, must relieve their pent-up anger. Thus out of their resentment, says Nietzsche, values are born as an imaginary revenge: "slave morality," with "the poisonous eye of ressentiment,"[5] says "no" to what it is not. This poisonous eye does not begin, as valuing might, by esteeming something for its intrinsic worth, but rather for the sake of devaluing what it is not and cannot be. It calls the strong "bad," and the weak "good" – thus "impotence which doesn't retaliate is being turned into

4 Ibid.
5 *On the Genealogy of Morals*, I. 11.

'goodness': timid baseness is being turned into 'humility'; sub-mission to people one hates is being turned into 'obedience'."[6]

But along with the birth of values come guilt, bad conscience, and asceticism. As goodness, humility, and the like are born, necessarily we come to view our "natural inclinations" with this same "evil eye,"[7] and our instincts to freedom, mastery, and power become the cause of bad conscience and guilt. This process takes another step when, in an expression of "unparalleled ressentiment,"[8] the troubled conscience turns to the ascetic life. Here, claims Nietzsche, there is a will which:

> wants to be master, not over something in life, but over life itself and its deepest, strongest, most profound conditions; here an attempt is made to use power to block the sources of the power; here, the green eye of spite turns on physiological growth itself, in particular the manifestation of this in beauty and joy; while satisfaction is *looked for* and found in failure, decay, pain, misfortune, ugliness, voluntary deprivation, destruction of self-hood, self-flagellation and self-sacrifice.[9]

This asceticism expresses, claims Nietzsche, "a will to nothing-ness, an aversion to life, a rebellion against the most fundamen-tal prerequisites of life."[10]

"This workshop where *ideals are fabricated* – it seems to me just to stink of lies."[11] The weak, full of resentment, wreak revenge through the invention of values which negate what they cannot be – strong. But after this invention, the lie involved in valuing humility and forbearance and charity over an original delight in human life and power is lost from view. Asceticism is, then, the final triumph of this "laboriously won *self-contempt* of man,"[12] concealing the original resentment and thus the true

6   *On the Genealogy of Morals*, I. 14.
7   *On the Genealogy of Morals*, II. 24.
8   *On the Genealogy of Morals*, III. 11.
9   Ibid.
10 *On the Genealogy of Morals*, III. 28.
11 *On the Genealogy of Morals*, I. 14.
12 *On the Genealogy of Morals*, III. 25.

genealogy of morality. And Christianity, "that most delicate flower of resentment,"[13] is the most complete form of this inversion. "I do not like the New Testament," says Nietzsche, "you have worked that out by now."[14]

Nietzsche gave too many hostages to fortune to have a reasonable expectation of being treated fairly. His aphoristic style encouraged the formulation of bold, polemical, witty maxims, which, in the manner of aphorisms, tend to exaggerate for effect. Out of context (and sometimes in context), these sayings can, in addition, seem highly misanthropic, misogynist and anti-Semitic – though it is doubtful that Nietzsche was any of these things. (Later uses of his term *Übermensch* are a further bar to sympathetic reading.) On top of all that, hints of Nietzsche's final mental breakdown can be detected – certainly with, and quite likely without, hindsight – especially in his later writings. (Entitling chapters in his *Ecce Homo* "Why I am so clever" and another, "Why I wrote such good books," could, of course, simply be a tease, but is probably not.) There is no shortage of pretexts for discounting the challenge Nietzsche poses.

But pretexts they are: for Nietzsche is a subtle, insightful, and profound psychologist. He cannot, and should not, be simply discounted. His purported genealogy of morals serves to indicate the character of a possible explanation of the genesis of moral judgment, and especially of agreement in moral judgment, even if we conclude it is more story than history. It is, to be sure, rather dubious as history. The "slaves" and "masters" of his story are not carefully drawn from originals, and it is doubtful that the early Christians and the Greeks, at whom their resentment is supposed to have been directed, were quite as they are imagined in Nietzsche's boldly drawn cartoons. But this is of very little account when we remember that Nietzsche's chief purpose in sketching a genealogy is to indicate how a key

[13]   M. Scheler's phrase in his useful study of Nietzsche, *Ressentiment*, trans. L. B. Coser and W. W. Holdheim (Milwaukee, 1998), 27.
[14]   *On the Genealogy of Morals*, III. 22.

but missing element in the relativist case might be provided – namely, an explanation of the very fact of moral judgment, and agreement in moral judgment, without making reference to truth.

Is this *the* explanation of such judgment? Well, Nietzsche's argument would need to be strengthened in countless ways if we were to be obliged to believe that. And even were we to conclude that it is *an* explanation (that is, part of a much wider explanatory account), further evidence and argument would be necessary. But it certainly serves a more modest, yet highly significant, purpose in simply casting doubt on the merits of the eighteenth-century faith in the moral subject by indicating what an alternative to that faith might be. Nietzsche shows us what a genealogy of moral judgment might look like, and in finding the very springs of moral judgment in the phenomena of resentment exposes recognizable psychological tendencies and patterns. At the very least, then, his genealogy of morals points to the naivety and innocence of the simple view that the only promising explanation of moral judgments, and of agreement in such judgments, is the existence and accessibility of moral truth, and it requires that such a view come to terms with the possibility of alternative genealogies.

Although the genealogists are, as we have noted, not united in the genealogy they advance, they cannot just be played off against each other. But can they be answered? Or rather, what elements in the genealogists' critique of moral judgment can or must be answered, if morality in general, or Christian morality in particular, is not to be held in disrepute? Here we need to make some careful distinctions, since to say that the genealogists threaten certain justifications of morality is not quite the same as saying that they threaten morality as such. Indeed, if we are to be clear about what Nietzsche intends, we shall have to notice that alongside his questioning of morality, Nietzsche also proposes what is, in effect, an alternative morality.

We can unravel these strands by underlining the point that the moral theories of the eighteenth century, in defending the authority of moral judgment, presupposed what we might term a "high anthropology." Theories such as Butler's viewed humankind as moral beings, imbued with a broadly reliable moral compass by which the subject could judge and direct his or her actions and to which appeal could be made in justifying these actions to the self and to other selves. And the possession of this moral compass was a special part of the dignity of human-kind in general, for it was in particular this faculty of moral judgment which, for example, distinguished humans from animals – or as we would say, from other animals.

In their different ways (and in the case of Darwin especially, with none of the relish which Nietzsche brings to the task), Nietzsche, Freud, Marx, and Darwin contest this account, and in contrast find what, from the perspective of the eighteenth century, seems to be a certain baseness in human life. Much righteous fury was aimed at what was thought of as Darwin's attempt, in his account of the descent of man, to make monkeys of us all; but the debasing of humanity, as it might be termed, was something at which the theories of all four aimed. Nietzsche's "improved" version of Luke 18: 14 – "He that humbleth him-self wants to be exalted"[15] – is just an instance of a general approach which looks with suspicion on the seemingly most noble of sentiments. And where Nietzsche finds the "will to power" concealed in the garb of humility, the others diagnose different, but no less base, motives or forces. Thus those human attributes that the eighteenth century had found most precious, namely the moral sentiments, and had made the basis for the defense of morality, look quite different in the light of the with-ering suspicions of alternative anthropologies.

Christianity is surely not under any obligation to repudiate these "lower anthropologies," however – at least insofar as these anthropologies remain what they are supposed to be, namely descriptive accounts of human life and psychology. Of course, these "debasing" anthropologies threaten a very par-ticular attempt to defend morality. But since such a defense is not essential to Christian ethics, in this respect Christianity can view the genealogists with equanimity. Indeed, far from

[15] F. Nietzsche, *Human, All Too Human*, trans. R. J. Hollingdale (Cambridge, 1986), para. 87.

repudiating anthropologies of the kind advanced by Nietzsche and the other nineteenth- and early twentieth-century "masters of suspicion," Christian ethics might simply find in them modern forms of its own authentic anthropological presuppositions.

The Augustinian account of the Fall, to which we referred in earlier chapters, paints what has often been thought to be a rather bleak picture of humanity. Be that as it may, an Augustinian Christianity has no very obvious reason to baulk at the genealogists' critiques of the optimistic anthropologies of the eighteenth century. Indeed Christianity should be suspicious of any contrary inclination to treat morality and conscience as if they are untainted relics of our pre-fallen lives. Christianity has an account of how humanity should be; as Augustine would have it, we are called to love God and one another in God. But this, very plainly, is not descriptive of how we are. Humankind may or may not be quite as conceived in, say, the pessimistic novels of the late nineteenth and early twentieth centuries, which bear witness to the influence of the period's unsentimental exploration of human life and motivations – the title of Zola's *La Bête Humaine* could serve to characterize the grim account of the human condition which is found as well in, say, Balzac, Tolstoy, and Conrad. But it is hard to see that the Christian moralist, presented with unsentimental accounts of human motives and the wretchedness of the human condition, should be either outraged or shocked.

The "debasing" anthropologies, taken as descriptions of human being, present no problem for Christianity then – unless, that is, Christianity turns away from these Augustinian presuppositions, and takes on a "high" view of humankind. Roman Catholicism sometimes seems to do just this, particularly in relation to its moral epistemology: thus, according to the recent Catechism, "Unintentional ignorance can diminish or even remove the imputability of a grave offence. But no one is deemed to be ignorant of the principles of the moral law, which are written in the conscience of every man."[16] And again: "sin tends

[16] *Catechism of the Catholic Church*, English trans. (London, 1994), para. 1860.

to reproduce and reinforce itself, but it cannot destroy the moral sense at its root."[17] Whatever is finally meant by these claims, they look very like the claims of the eighteenth-century moralists, with their high view of humankind. Augustinian Christianity will repudiate such views as, amongst other things, contrary to a serious phenomenology of our moral plight, which consists not only in an unwillingness to do the good, but also in our inability to will what we know to be good, our difficulties in knowing it, and our willful misconstructions of what we might be said to know. Just insofar as the eighteenth century seemed to presuppose the ready availability of moral truth and the innocence of the moral sentiments, Christian moral philosophy has many reasons to prefer the nineteenth.

Of course, we are leaving out of account for the moment the question to which we will return to in the next chapter. What should be said in reply to the relativism of which Hobbes's views are a precursor? All we have done for now is to point out the weaknesses in a particular strategy for answering relativism. This strategy seems to depend on what I called a "high" anthropology, and in this respect it is at odds with the claims of the genealogists (and of Augustine). Christian moral thought may or may not need a reply to relativism, but, so I have alleged, it certainly shouldn't reply with a highly problematic insistence on the merits of a high anthropology; thus it can and should be willing to learn from Nietzsche, Marx, Darwin, and Freud.

But at this point we have to put down a marker, since, as already mentioned, the genealogists and their followers were by no means scrupulous in sticking to description, and steering clear of prescription. And this threatens to confuse the issue. To say how humans are is one thing; to say how they should be is another. And whilst Nietzsche's account of human motivation may be valuable as a contribution to a descriptive anthropology (and one with which Christian ethics may and can come to terms), his critique of Christian ideals, based on a prescription of a particular and quite different conception of what it is to be human, is not.

[17]   *Catechism of the Catholic Church*, para. 1865.

The possibility of confusion on this point is increased by the fact that Nietzsche doesn't openly propose an alternative "moral code," though this is, in effect, exactly what he does. The same sort of confusion is possible in relation to Darwin – or more accurately, Darwinism. Darwinism has often been thought not only to provide an account of how humans are, but also to license various prescriptions as to how they should be. Thus, to point to an outstanding example, the nineteenth-century English thinker Herbert Spencer, seems to take a scientific account of an evolutionary struggle for existence as a vindication of social and moral principles which reflect the same competitive spirit. This move has had a continuing appeal (especially to successful capitalists), even if the classic answer seems sufficient – namely, that nature has its business and we have ours, but that we are under no obligation to run ours along the very same lines.

Nietzsche is not dealt with in quite that way, since there is no mere sleight of hand in his commending what is, in effect, an alternative morality to the Christian code which he finds contemptible. As has been noticed by certain commentators, Nietzsche's obsessive concern with unmasking Christianity shows a remarkable prescience, since he discerns in it something which could not easily have been perceived in the worldly versions of Christianity favored by the liberal Protestantism with which he was familiar. This worldly Christianity was contemptible in Nietzsche's (and Kierkegaard's) eyes, as no more than bourgeois respectability. But despite its liberal defenders, Nietzsche discerned in Christianity something worthy of his persistent and insightful attention – and that was precisely an anthropology absolutely at odds with his own conception of true humanity.

So, whether or not his genealogy is good as genealogy, and whether or not we accept his account of how humans are, Nietzsche invites us to share his distaste for Christianity's conception of how humans should be. Christianity, as he conceives it, asks us to commit ourselves to principles of sympathy, solidarity, and community – and thus to a particular way of being human. The Greeks of his imagining and of his normative anthropology are altogether different. For these Greeks, to be human is essentially to live "like strong winds" – "to live above them [i.e., the unclean, the slaves, the herd], neighbours to eagles, neighbours to snow, neighbours to the sun."[18] We can, if we wish, call this a rejection of morality, and this is what Nietzsche's own phrase "beyond good and evil" suggests. The genealogy of morals, exposing the nature of the "workshop in which ideals were fabricated," is supposed to liberate us to exercise those vital instincts which have been constrained by the morality of the herd. (Napoleon is held up as an, albeit problematic, "late-born" exemplar of "the ancient ideal."[19]) But whether we call this a rejection of morality or not, there is here undoubtedly a normative and competing anthropology – a competing conception of what it is to be human and a quasi-prophetic call to realize it. It is this normative conception of what is truly human which underlies Nietzsche's charge that "morality itself was the danger of dangers."[20]

Morality, Christian morality, is very definitely the "danger of dangers" for this celebration of humanity's vital instincts and will to power. As Barth puts it, in Christ this creed meets its utter negation; the pretended superman is taught that "In this crucified, and therefore in fellowship with this mean and painful host of His people, he has ... to see his salvation, and his true humanity in the fact that he belongs to Him and therefore to them."[21] This is, very plainly, a clash between radically opposed anthropologies, and a clash which Christianity has every reason to expose and confront. Indeed, the two twentieth-century Christian ethicists to whose work we turn in the next chapter both agreed with Nietzsche on this very point – namely that Christianity finds itself in contention with his and many other secular notions of how humans should be.

The genealogists exposed the moral subject to a critical scrutiny which could not simply be gainsaid. Thus no appeal to the

---

[18] F. Nietzsche, *Thus Spoke Zarathustra*, trans. A. del Caro (Cambridge, 2006), 76.
[19] *On the Genealogy of Morals*, I. 16.
[20] *On the Genealogy of Morals*, Preface, 6.
[21] K. Barth, *Church Dogmatics*, III. 2, trans. H. Knight et al. (Edinburgh, 1960), 241.

subject as the source of moral authority could ever again seem as uncontentious as it did in the previous period. So it is that the problem of relativism emerged sharper and fresher at the beginning of the twentieth century than it had appeared even perhaps in the midst of the conflicts of the seventeenth. Christianity needed not only to re-examine its conception of what it is to be human, and perhaps to delineate this view in its very particularity. It needed also to consider again how this conception might be commended or proclaimed.

7

Karl Barth and John Paul II: The Rediscovery of Christian Ethics

Where Christianity gained cultural prestige and wide influence, the Christian way of life could come to be regarded as simply commanded by reason or common sense – especially so if Christianity had practiced some accommodation itself in gaining this pre-eminence. However that may be, the identification of Christian ethics as a matter of simple and unquestionable norms became increasingly unacceptable, not only to the self-conscious secularism of certain nineteenth-century thinkers, but also to Christian thinkers, such as Kierkegaard, who thought that Christianity's distinctiveness and challenge had been lost in this rapprochement. Nietzsche's attack on Christianity only served to underline the particularity of Christianity's understanding of what it is to be human and to live well.

A sense of the distinctiveness of Christian life and thought is common to two of the twentieth century's most powerful and influential reflections on the nature of Christian morality. These two accounts stand like bookends at the beginning and at the close of the period, both stressing the particularity and counter-cultural character of authentic Christian witness. And both, in stressing this distinctiveness, have to come to terms with the perennial question of the relationship between theology and moral theology, on the one hand, and philosophy, reason, and ethics, on the other. Just because of the supposed distinctiveness of Christian thought, this question cannot be handled with a quick reassurance about the essential agreement between the two

Karl Barth, the century's greatest Protestant theologian, was initially led to develop his influential restatement of a Christian orthodoxy against the dominant liberal strain of Christian apologetics by the particular crisis of 1914. In that year, "ninety-three German intellectuals issued a terrible manifesto identifying themselves before all the world with the war policy of Kaiser Wilhelm II.... And to my dismay," Barth wrote, "among the signatories I discovered the names of almost all my German teachers."[1] Enlightened, liberated, cultured Europe was about to tear itself apart in a war for which there was no readily identifiable, let alone manifestly just, cause – and the liberal theological establishment had nothing to contribute except a call for loyalty to the fatherland. Barth was led to examine the very foundations of the theological approach which he had imbibed, and he concluded that liberal theology was essentially bankrupt. It sought in the Bible only a confirmation and completion of human thought; doing this, it followed predictably that it could have very little to add to such thought. But according to Barth, as he went back to the Bible, it does not offer confirmation and completion, but instead challenges human culture, self-understanding, and consciousness. The task then, for Christian theology properly conceived, and for Christian ethics in particular, is to expound the bearing of Christian doctrine on human life. As he would say in one of the sharp, clear slogans which appealed to him (and to which we will return presently): "Dogmatics itself is ethics; and ethics is also dogmatics."[2] As Europe drifted from one great war to another, Barth's sense of the need for clarity in regard to the particular demands of Christian action and witness did not diminish.

At the end the century, John Paul II, perhaps the most influential Roman Catholic thinker of the period, also voiced a strong sense of the counter-cultural character of Christianity. That Christianity should be at odds with the communism of the post-war Soviet bloc, including the Pope's native Poland, is perhaps not surprising – Christian thought has always had regard for the importance of the individual before God, a regard which has made it critical of totalitarianism in its various guises, and

---

[1]   Cited in E. Busch, *Karl Barth* (London, 1976), 81.
[2]   K. Barth, *Church Dogmatics*, I. 2, trans. G. Thomson and H. Knight (Edinburgh, 1956), 793.

explains its historical connection with the emergence of political liberalism. What is more striking, perhaps, is that in addition to this standard criticism John Paul develops a more wide-ranging critique of modernity, directed as much at the West as at the East. Of course, just as Christianity has suspected totalitarianism of neglecting the individual, so it has often suspected liberalism of overlooking the common good and thus of protecting the individual as the expense of society, and this is an important element in John Paul's interrogation of life under modern capitalism. But John Paul also finds, in the secularism which has become the underlying creed of many modern political systems, a fundamental lack of respect for life, and it is here especially that he emphasizes the distinctiveness of the claims of Christian morality.

Though John Paul II and Karl Barth both emphasize the distinctiveness of Christian ethics, on the matter of apologetics they seem to part company. Albeit that he is sensitive to the particular questions and debates of the period, John Paul offers what is essentially a restatement of a natural law approach. Christianity may be the particular guardian of certain moral truths, but a theological ethic builds on and takes further a morality which is, in its foundations, the common possession of all reasonable people. Barth, on the other hand, is fundamentally uninterested in apologetics, and doubts the availability of neutral ground on which Christian claims may build. Thus John Paul not only proclaims the distinctiveness of a Christian anthropology, but at the same time holds to its reasonableness against the challenges of skepticism and relativism. Karl Barth, however, consciously repudiates apologetics if apologetics is understood as an attempt to commend Christianity to human thought, and is more concerned with the exposition of Christian belief than with its reasonableness. We shall return to this difference between them when they have each had a chance to speak for themselves.

When Barth declares that "dogmatics itself is ethics; and ethics is also dogmatics," he is saying something which is widely taken for granted, although, of course, the language is unfamiliar in common parlance. The man or woman in the street expects the theologian to have a view, and probably a quite particular view, on ethical questions, even if he or she could offer no very explicit account of what gives the theologian a particular interest or expertise in the matter. So it is that a TV news programme, just as it looks for a stockbroker or banker to comment on a change in interest rates, may seek someone with a religious perspective to comment on proposals to change the law relating to marriage or on the rights and wrongs of going to war. But what account can we give of the relationship between Christian belief and ethical judgment which is commonly supposed to exist? Barth's position can perhaps be best understood by contrasting it with two views which do not relate doctrine and ethics in the way he does.

The first view might be thought of as standing to the left. In the spirit of Kant's *Religion Within the Bounds of Reason Alone* it takes the slogan "dogmatics is ethics" in what Barth would regard as a reductive sense, converting the dogmas of Christian faith into symbolic representations of moral truths. Matthew Arnold once said that "the true meaning of religion is ... not simply morality but morality touched by emotion," but Barth does not intend to endorse any reductive account of doctrine. As Barth would see it, such a position has little to offer to contemporary culture other than a reflection of that culture's own leading assumptions, refracted through religious sentiments.

Though Barth is not saying that dogmatics is ethics and nothing but ethics since, after all, dogmatics is about God, he is nonetheless insistent that it is ethics and is essentially so, and in saying this he protests against another position, which we might think of as on the right. This view is not reductive of doctrine, but limits doctrine's significance in such a way as to achieve much the same result – doctrine is conceived of as concerned with the contemplation of the eternal, and moral teaching is thought of as concerned with the temporal. In popular terms it is the "keep religion out of politics" view of the relation between theology and ethics, which says, in effect, that Christian doctrine is all about metaphysical or transcendent reality. Christian faith is thought to involve commitment to particular beliefs, perhaps also to the cultivation of personal holiness or personal sanctification; but it does not compel any commitment to morality in a wider, worldly sense. As we have noted, the "culprit," as both Barth and Bonhoeffer would see it, in foisting this misconception on the church is principally Luther: his reconfiguring of the distinction between two kingdoms, and his suspicion of morality as a technique aimed at the achievement of righteousness before God were two of the elements which contributed to a sharp separation of doctrine and ethics in Protestant life and thought, and hence to the quietism of German churches even under the Nazis.

While theological slogans about dogmatics and ethics may not make the pulse race, the urgency and sharpness with which Barth proclaimed and argued for these positions (even issuing one rebuke to an erring theologian under the title "Nein!") had to do, not with the niceties of theological distinctions, but with the need for utter clarity if the church in Germany and elsewhere was to fulfill its duty in opposing tyranny and oppression. The church, Barth protested, needed to recall that theology is at one and the same time theoretical and practical. Dogma really is dogma, but this dogma is also, as a matter of fact, of practical and existential significance. This is not, notice, a necessary truth about religion in general, but a contingent truth about the actual content of Christianity. Theology might have been about God alone, and his being and essence; but the story recounted in the Bible is a story of a God who calls, summons, and commands humankind. God's being as it is revealed in the Bible is, we might say, being in action, and, specifically in relation to humankind, is expressed in his claiming them for a way of life which cannot be exhaustively characterized by reference to a sphere of personal or private holiness.

How, then, should this claiming of humankind by God be characterized? Although Barth gives a general answer to this question, it is the burden of what he says that exactly what is needed is not a general answer, but rather careful and detailed theological reflection on the countless and diverse situations in which humans act. In general terms one could say, as common sense might expect, that Christian ethics will take its shape and content from the biblical story. That is to say, according to

Barth, Christian ethics must take its bearings from the life, death, and resurrection of Jesus Christ, in which is revealed threefold knowledge of God and humankind as Creator and creature, reconciler and sinner, redeemer and child of God. Christian ethics reflects on the implications of living in the light of that knowledge. Life lived thus will involve our looking back in reverence to the created order which the resurrection affirms, and forwards in hope to the eschatological transformation of the created order of which the resurrection also speaks; to live so, is just what it means for humans to take seriously the nature and character of God's saving action in history. But what this means in particular will require detailed reflection on God's action and calling as they are revealed, not only in this history of salvation, but also in the continuation of that history in the present.

Barth's insistence that Christian ethics begins with Jesus Christ has, by the way, nothing to do with what we might call "biblicism," which has certainly been a popular way for many Christians to approach ethical issues in the modern period. Biblicism is the view that ethics should, in a very narrow and specific sense, be biblical – meaning typically that it should be based on biblical texts, such as the Ten Commandments, or the Sermon on the Mount, or what Paul says about the treatment of women, or whatever seems pertinent to the matter in hand. The theological objection to this way of doing ethics is just that, in its tendency to treat ethics as a matter of various commands and dictates, it neglects the possibility of understanding the moral law as not merely a set of random obligations but a coherent whole – which is to say, of course, that biblicism, though it is certainly solemn, is really not very serious. Biblicism, in other words, pretends to earnestness in its ethics, but its occasionalism (i.e., its treating of the commandments as a collection of occasional dictates), denies Christian ethics the coherence which comes from taking its starting point not from the Bible in this narrow sense, but from the being and nature of God as that being and nature are disclosed in the story of salvation. It is, after all, this story, and not the giving of detached ethical instruction, which the Bible is about.

The distinctiveness of Christian ethics can be asserted as a general truth, but is, of course, only finally demonstrated in the sort of detailed reflections on friendship, marriage, war, peace, death, and so on, which are found in Barth's great work, *Church Dogmatics*. In this work Barth concludes his sequential treatment of the central doctrines of the Christian faith (namely the doctrines of creation, reconciliation, and redemption), with specific sections aimed at explicating the claim that "dogmatics itself is ethics," drawing from each of these doctrines their implications for various aspects of human life. However, even without attending to the particularities of each of these treatments, it is nonetheless possible to follow Barth in his drawing attention to the most fundamentally distinctive theme of Christian anthropology in contrast to what he regards as the quite different anthropologies of modernity. To use another of Barth's slogans, according to Christian anthropology to be human is to be with and for the other, whereas it is, he contends, characteristic of dominant and competing anthropologies to understand human being as a being without, or even against, the other.

A theological anthropology, so Barth asserts, must be founded on Christology – that is to say, for Christian thought Christ is the "source of our knowledge of the nature of man as created by God."[3] In the light of this source, true human being is properly understood as a being for others. To be human is be in relationship or encounter. It is constitutive of our humanity, in other words, that where there is an "I" there is also a "Thou." Fellowship and community belong to our being, to its essence. This, Barth says, is "the secret of humanity."[4] And it is a secret hidden from, or denied, by many competing understandings of humanity which "overlook the fact of [man's] being in fellowship, and see him for himself, constructing him in terms of an abstract 'I am' in which others are not yet or no longer included."[5]

[3]   *Church Dogmatics*, III. 2, trans. H. Knight et al. (Edinburgh, 1960), 41.
[4]   *Church Dogmatics*, III. 2. 274.
[5]   *Church Dogmatics*, III. 2. 243.

As we have seen, it is, of course, Nietzsche who is the most outspoken prophet of this other view. Nietzsche commends for our emulation not man as a social animal but man as an eagle of azure isolation, triumphing in his will, strength, and independence, heedless of the claims of others – the hero of Nietzsche's thought is, then, Napoleon or Cesare Borgia, but not the petty man of everyday life, still less the "pale Galilean" who has corrupted the world with his sympathy and his humility.

Now if these two conceptions are set side by side, it might be thought that Nietzsche stands as something of a lonely exception to the general tendency, following Aristotle, to understand human being as social, although in certain versions of existentialism (such as that associated with Camus, for example) an admiration for Nietzsche's conception of human being can be recognized. Is it not the Christian model of the truly human, that is to say, which is widely admired and accepted, the Nietzschean account which is denied and rejected?

According to Barth, however, Nietzsche's account of human being as being without is not, in fact, quite such an exception. Nietzsche's construction of humanity "in terms of an abstract 'I am'" is, rather, the epitome of a longer project of thought. Nietzsche may be, as Barth puts it, the "most consistent ... prophet of humanity without the fellow-man," but he is not alone. In much of the Western philosophical tradition, in metaphysics and in morals, the other has seemed questionable and a problem in various senses, whereas the self has been secure and central. And life "without the fellow-man," whatever liberalism's intentions, has become a characteristic feature of modern existence – the increase in "bowling alone," to take an evocative expression of the phenomenon,[6] suggests that liberalism has rather served to turn the individual from society than towards it. This turn we might find mirrored in social practices of a less trivial kind. Thus in medicine, which is increasingly shaped by respect for one of the chief goods of modernity, namely

[6]   R. D. Putnam, *Bowling Alone: The Collapse and Revival of American Community*, new edn. (New York, 2000).

autonomy, the receiving of care (by the dying, the infirm, and the handicapped), is often represented and experienced as essentially demeaning – just as the Nietzschean hero would, no doubt, regard it. Civic disengagement and individual isolation seem to go hand in hand.

If Christian ethics has then, as might be expected, a distinctive form and content, expressed in very general terms in its conception of what it is to be human, how might such ethics be commended to the world? Barth is uninterested in apologetics, at least as apologetics are often conceived, and in this attitude claims to be true to the Bible. The Bible, so he contends, does not confirm and complete human thought, but challenges it. The Word of God does not base itself on human culture, self-understanding, and consciousness, but instead judges culture, self-understanding, and consciousness. Certainly it does not satisfy criteria of reasonableness stipulated by its critics. And the task of theology is certainly not to justify the Word of God, let alone to judge it. Its task is to expound and explicate it. Theological ethics is no different in this respect – it describes, not defends, the practical significance for human life and action of the life and action of God.

John Paul II has, as we shall see, a different approach to apologetics, but like Barth a strong sense of the distinctive message of Christianity to the world. And just as Christianity, properly understood, was bound to express this distinctive message in sharply opposing fascist tyranny and communist oppression, so after the collapse of the Soviet empire and "the end of history" as Fukuyama termed it, it was bound to offer a critique of the individualist materialism of modern capitalism. In his encyclicals (letters addressed by popes to the worldwide church), John Paul paints a sometimes very bleak picture of modern life and culture as in the grip of all sorts of false ideas and values. Yet at the same time, and here unlike Karl Barth, he maintains a certain faith and optimism in the possibility of arguing the world out its errors. In this sense he offers an alternative strategy to Barth's repudiation of apologetics, and instead can be regarded as providing a restatement of a natural law ethic. Two of his encyclicals – *Evangelium Vitae* and *Veritatis Splendor* – illustrate well the two strains in his thought.

Evangelium Vitae is a sharp expression of John Paul's sense of the need to preserve the particularity of Christian practice in the face of what he sees as the crisis of modern culture. That crisis consists in the "vast array of threats to human life," of which the threats to life at its beginning and end are the chief concern of the encyclical. According to John Paul, "choices once unanimously considered criminal and rejected by the common moral sense are gradually becoming socially acceptable."[7] Indeed some of these choices, such as abortion, "tend no longer to be considered as 'crimes'" but "paradoxically ... assume the nature of 'rights' to the point that the State is called upon to give them legal recognition and to make them available through the free services of health-care personnel."[8] What makes this the more striking is that these attacks are most often "carried out in the heart of and with the complicity of the family – the family which by its nature is called to be the 'sanctuary of life'."[9]

What is important for the encyclical, however, is not the matter of abortion as such, but rather that the social acceptance of these attacks on life points to a wider attitude, and to a "problem which exists at the cultural, social and political level."[10] The problem is that, "fostered by powerful cultural, economic and political currents which encourage an idea of society excessively concerned with efficiency," there has come to be "a war of the powerful against the weak," "a conspiracy against life," and "a veritable 'culture of death'."[11] It is a question, then, "in a certain sense, of the 'moral conscience' of society," which as a result of the "eclipse of the sense of God and of man," "not only ... tolerates or fosters behaviour contrary to life, but also ... encourages the 'culture of death', creating and consolidating actual 'structures of sin' which go against life."[12]

---

[7]   John Paul II, *Evangelium Vitae* (London, 1995), 4.
[8]   *Evangelium Vitae*, 11.
[9]   Ibid.
[10]   *Evangelium Vitae*, 18.
[11]   *Evangelium Vitae*, 12.
[12]   *Evangelium Vitae*, 24.

The "moral conscience, both individual and social," is in "mortal danger," at risk of "confusing good and evil, precisely in relation to the fundamental right to life."[13] In the face of the confusion and the resulting culture of death, the church is engaged in "a great struggle" evoked, in the conclusion to the encyclical, in the highly charged imagery of the book of Revelation.[14]

Veritatis Splendor, an earlier encyclical, also has a high sense of moral crisis. Indeed, it might be thought to paint an even darker picture, just because its concern is not with the errors of secular thought but with the way in which those errors are being taken up even by Christians. "In the present circumstances," warns the Pope, the fundamental truths of the church's teaching "risk being distorted and denied,"[15] as a secular mentality affects

> even the attitudes and behaviour of Christians, whose faith is weakened and loses its character as a new and original criterion for thinking and acting in personal, family and social life. In a widely dechristianized culture, the criteria employed by believers themselves in making judgments and decisions often appear extraneous or even contrary to those of the Gospel. It is urgent then that Christians should rediscover the newness of the faith and its power to judge a prevalent and all-intrusive culture.[16]

Yet for all his sense of a cultural crisis so pervasive that even Christianity may be engulfed in it, John Paul at the very same time holds to the view that the central truths which have been, or are in danger of being, eclipsed are nonetheless available to reason. Our culture may be confused, and Christians may themselves come to share in these confusions, and thus both Christians and non-Christians may be led to turn away from moral reality or truth. But under the careful tutorship of reason

13 Ibid.
14 *Evangelium Vitae*, 104.
15 John Paul II, *Veritatis Splendor* (London, 1993), 4.
16 *Veritatis Splendor*, 88.

and argument there can be a rediscovery of "the rational – and thus universally understandable and communicable ... moral norms belonging to the sphere of the natural moral law."[17] These norms are ones which have traditionally been authoritative in societies, religious or otherwise; they are expressed, for example, in many of the Ten Commandments: do not commit murder, do not lie, do not commit adultery, do not steal.

So what is the confusion which has led modernity into error, but from which it can be saved by right reason? The central confusion, according to John Paul II, concerns the relationship between freedom and moral truth. In various ways, modernity has come to oppose these two, and to think that true freedom is found in forms of moral subjectivism which invite us to create our own values. Nietzsche saw himself, of course, as the prophet of such a creative freedom.

However, this approach is wrong on two counts, according to John Paul II. First, just because there are truths to which we must be responsible, and second, because to be responsible to them is no loss of freedom. The truths to which we must be responsible are those expressed in the laws to which we have just referred and which are known to reason; and being responsible to them is no loss of freedom just because these laws, discovered by human reason, direct us to our true good. In obeying these laws we find true liberty and authentic existence. Where these laws are set aside, however, preference and desire become the sole arbiters of private action, and naked power the sole determinant of public life.

The false exaltation of freedom is thus highly dangerous, as *Veritatis Splendor* warns and "as history demonstrates," for "a democracy without values easily turns into open or thinly disguised totalitarianism."[18] Certainly the assumption that moral relativism offers some sort of justification for pluralism and tolerance is mistaken, even if it is a popular thought. Indeed, it is not a thought which can survive a moment's reflection. If moral beliefs cannot be satisfactorily justified it is difficult to

[17]   *Veritatis Splendor*, 58.
[18]   *Veritatis Splendor*, 152.

see how that means that some moral values, such as values of tolerance and pluralism, are thereby vindicated. Rather, as John Paul II warns, a breakdown in belief in moral truth leads as easily to oppression as it does to tolerance. If there is no moral truth by which our actions may be measured, then there is no more force in the claim that we should respect difference than in the thought that we should eradicate it. This is a matter of logic, but also of experience – the history of the twentieth century does not suggest that liberation from the "dogmas" of morality produces a kinder or gentler world.

At the end of the century then, John Paul, highly conscious of the skeptical tendencies of modern thought, and concerned at the direction of social policy, attempts to restate the essence and core of the natural law tradition. How successful is this strategy?

John Paul II is surely right to attack the rather lazy moral skepticism which is found in our culture. (Amongst undergraduates, instances of this lazy skepticism about truth and values are usually very quickly abandoned if one awards low marks to an essay on the grounds that that is how one "felt" about it.) But even a more thoughtful skepticism needs probing. Though, as we have noted, relativism in relation to moral beliefs has a long history, its status as a good explanation of the phenomenon of moral disagreement within and between societies is not beyond question. Some critics of moral relativism doubt the existence of the deep and fundamental disagreements which it tends to assume – after all, radical differences of practice can arise from common moral values. (Thus, you might honor the dead, say, by dancing on their graves as much as by maintaining a hushed silence in their vicinity.) But even where the existence of deep disagreements is admitted, and these disagreements are associated with identified social groupings or historical epochs, the relativist needs to show the impossibility of their resolution by rational deliberation – without that, such disagreements merely show that there is indeed a plurality of moral views. But to establish that moral disagreements are not open to resolution is by no means a straightforward matter, and influential thinkers, such as Alasdair MacIntyre, have contended that the case for relativism often depends on presupposing standards of rational justification which few or no beliefs could satisfy, even about straightforward empirical and observable matters.

Referred to as "anti-foundationalists," these thinkers acknowledge that moral beliefs cannot be derived from some neutral, self-evident foundation, but necessarily arise and belong within particular traditions of thought and enquiry. They argue, however, that these traditions are not beyond question, but may show themselves to be adequate or inadequate as they are subject to articulation and development, and as part of that process show an ability, or otherwise, to respond to questioning from other traditions. This is not the same as showing one proof in algebra to be valid, and another to be invalid. But beliefs about all sorts of things can be reasonable or unreasonable without being capable of demonstration.

This is a line of reasoning to which John Paul II would be sympathetic, and there is no doubt that his insistence on the knowability of the moral law is a powerful statement of an influential position. Yet we should also notice that his understanding of our contemporary moral plight, combined with his prescription for our rescue, presents something of a paradox. The paradox can be indicated in a question: how can it be that we find ourselves in the grip of "a culture of death" which offends, so he believes, against the most basic of moral truths, just when the truths against which it offends are said to be available as "an imperishable spark" to right reason and conscience?[19] Either reason has less power than he sometimes maintains, or the existence of this culture is something of a mystery.

Alongside his belief in the ability of unaided human reason to rescue us from our plight, at other times John Paul seems acutely aware that the "gospel of life" in fact rests on particular Christian moral convictions – as Karl Barth believes. This is not to say that reason is redundant and useless. Far from it. It is doubtless the case that in relation to all sorts of moral questions there is confusion and inconsequence and thus that careful

---

[19]   *Veritatis Splendor*, 59.

reasoning and argument may resolve certain disagreements. But it is one thing to think that argument may serve from time to time to amend certain moral positions and claims, another to believe that reason alone can establish something like a general universal ethic which expresses the central convictions of a truly Christian anthropology.

If it cannot, this is, theologically speaking, hardly surprising. For as Barth points out, the natural law viewpoint depends, in effect, on a view of the Fall as "merely relative and quantitative," as if humankind has fallen to a degree but at root retains a grasp on knowledge of God and of his will, and retains too a disposition to do that will. But this, so Barth and other Augustinians would suggest, is a shallow account of human sin, behind which Barth suspects a shallow account of the nature of God's grace. Reason will have its place, purpose, and role – but for both philosophical and theological reasons, it seems doubtful that it will establish as wholly reasonable an ethic with the rich content for which Barth and others contend.

It seems likely that this debate about the validity of the natural law tradition (and hence about the particularity of Christian ethics), just doesn't admit of an answer which favors one side wholly at the expense of the other. Both sides are surely protecting positions which are highly defensible. The skeptical side alerts us to what has been called the "thickness" of morality, Christian or otherwise, and the need to locate moral codes and concepts in traditions, practices, and forms of life.[20] The natural law tradition is interested in identifying what is "thin" in Christian morality, in the sense of what is founded not in the specific and thick tradition, but in our common humanity and reason. Arguments on either side have been and will be advanced – but it seems highly unlikely that either side can land a knock-out blow.

---

[20] The terms are used by, amongst others, M. Walzer, *Thick and Thin: Moral Arguments at Home and Abroad* (Notre Dame, 1994).

8

History in the Present: Genetics, Philosophy, and Christian Life

In the twenty or thirty years after the ending of the Second World War by the use of nuclear weapons, it was the awesome powers delivered into human hands by modern physics which fascinated and frightened the popular imagination. Before the turn of the century, however, the power to instill fear and awe passed firmly to the biological sciences – the birth of Dolly the cloned sheep in 1997 and the completion of the map of the human genome in 2003 provided emblematic moments when developments in biology and its application impressed themselves on public consciousness. Biotechnology (literally, the technology of life), seemed to present new and dramatic possibilities and powers. These possibilities have been the stuff of anxious debate and discussion in newspapers and on radio and television; in fiction and film they have served as material for, typically, dystopian fables. It suffices to mention Margaret Atwood's novel of 2003, *Oryx and Crake*, or the film *The Island*, made in 2005, with Ewan McGregor and Scarlet Johannson. In Atwood's story, the world has been devastated by the unanticipated consequences of experiments aimed at xenotransplantation – that is, the modification of non-human animals (in this case pigs), for the sake of developing organs for use in humans. In *The Island*, the same desire for replacements for failing organs lies behind the nightmarish scenario which the film conjures up – a private corporation offers the very rich the opportunity to maintain, ready for use in case of need, a real-life clone as the perfect source for new body parts. Both serve as examples of the general sense that biology and its applications pose pressing and worrying questions for the future of human life – and also witness to a common perception that what drives our appetite for the development of biotechnology is chiefly a concern for human health.

In a very striking essay written more than thirty years ago, Hans Jonas, a philosopher much concerned with the biological sciences (as well as being a noted historian of ancient thought), attempted to identify what was new and challenging in the emerging applications of biology.[1] The newness of biotechnology, so he argues, was just that for the first time we are forced to reckon with the mutability of nature, and even human nature. Previously human action took place against the backdrop of a given world. Nature was the context in which we acted, not itself the object of our actions. Then the facts of human existence were "ordained," but now, so he contends, they can be accepted or rejected. Here, however, is just where, according to Jonas, we find ourselves in difficulties. The category which might bring us up short and serve to govern and constrain our actions, namely the category of the "sacred," is the very category which the triumph of science has destroyed. Religion, says Jonas, is no longer available to us as "a sole-determining force." "Now," he says, "we shiver in the nakedness of a nihilism in which near-omnipotence is paired with near emptiness, greatest capacity with knowing least what for."[2]

As our brief history arrives at the present day, Jonas's diagnosis of our circumstances has considerable pertinence. He seems to present us with a rather stark and, for religion, a somewhat wistful either/or. Either we can appeal to the category of the sacred to constrain and govern our use of biotechnology, or we are left with the more limited resources of everyday common sense and prudence. The wistfulness is that what could light our way (namely religious belief), is, at least as many of our contemporaries would see it, only available to us as a fond (or not so fond) memory.

---

[1] H. Jonas, "Technology and Responsibility: Reflections on the New Tasks of Ethics," in *Philosophical Essays* (Chicago, 1974), 3–20.
[2] Jonas, "Technology and Responsibility," 20.

For the time being we should leave the sense of wistfulness to one side – as we have said before, the task of this book is to expound the ethical significance of Christian belief, not to address directly the merits of that belief as such. Whether what Christianity seems to require of us is thought of as a piece of quaint nostalgia or as a present and pressing imperative is not necessarily determined within ethical thought itself. But the character and nature of that requirement is very definitely ethics' proper subject; and what Christian ethics asks of us in the sphere of the application of biotechnology is something we must now seek to clarify. What then shall we say? Does Christianity have a particular contribution to make to this issue, of such contemporary importance? What analysis does it offer, and furthermore, how distinctive is its account of the issues we confront and of how we should think about them?

No matter whether or not Christianity may have something distinctive to say in this regard, Christian reflection on biotechnology will need to start with clarifications which should serve as common ground amongst those who are concerned with these matters. These clarifications address certain misunderstandings of science and certain inadequacies in moral thought. Whether it is a Christian analysis of the issues posed by biotechnology or otherwise, it needs to advance from solid scientific and philosophical grounds. Where it does not, there is a risk of two rather too familiar phenomena in this area – we might think of them as the ringing of alarm bells where there is no fire (where bad science leads us to worry about fearful prospects which are totally fantastic), or the silence of the alarms where there really is a fire (where bad ethics finds no cause for concern in relation to what are genuine possibilities). In one case the warnings are misconceived, and in the other the consolations are worthless. Only when we have understood what the issues are, scientifically and ethically, will we be in a position to consider what theology may have to say, and whether this differs, and if so, how, from other contributions.

Those who seek to spread alarm at the possibilities presented by the new biology and its applications have, one might say, as their stock in trade for sending shivers down the spine, the cloning of dictators. When Dolly had just been cloned, it was quite remarkable how many discussions on radio and television would begin with news of the birth of a sheep, and move very quickly to the supposedly fearful prospect of a rogue scientist producing a clone of Hitler – as if the work on sheep was but a preliminary to the real project!

There are doubtless all sorts of reasons for not cloning Hitler, but fear of the havoc his clone would wreak need not be amongst them, for such a fear probably arises from a mistaken understanding of the relationship between genes and character. There are, of course, genes for certain simple traits (even if that statement itself merits some qualifications) – it is, after all, the relationship between a certain gene or genes, and a certain trait or traits, on which depends the long-standing human success in modifying animals and plants by selective breeding. These modifications are however, of relatively simple traits – someone breeding dogs, for example, may select for length or color of coat, or even for temperament. It is, of course, more than likely then, that Hitler's twin brother, whether created alongside him in the womb, or after him in a test tube, would, as his clone, resemble him in certain respects. But that his clone would be destined to be an anti-Semitic militarist, bringing death and destruction on millions, is not itself written into the genes. The relationship between nature and nurture in the creation of character is far more subtle than any such genetic determinism seems to allow – a point which makes a nonsense of nearly all the stories, beloved of newspapers, about "genes for" just about everything under the sun, from divorce to dishonesty.

Scientists themselves have some share in perpetrating the confusions which return to be used against them. "We are our genes" is a slogan which has doubtless done sterling service for advocates of the importance of funding work on the frontiers of biology and its applications. But taken seriously as an account of what makes me me, with its suggestion that genes are the all-important and sufficient ground and essence of who I am, it is plain false – as any identical twin would testify. Genes influence who we are, but for most important traits don't determine it – and very certainly not in ways which should cause us to lie awake at night worrying about the cloning of dictators.

If it is sometimes a questionable understanding of science which leads to the sounding of alarms when there really is no fire at all, it is poor ethics which is typically responsible for the opposite phenomenon, and the silence of the alarm bells even when there is a fire. For our purposes we need to notice (but, I will suggest, then discount), the false reassurances which come from much bioethics.

One of the dominant strands in bioethics derives from an ethical theory which is often labeled "consequentialism." Consequentialism has been astonishingly influential and is manifestly very appealing as a basis for thinking about morals. It therefore needs to be understood and reckoned with. It is however, the basis for the false assurances I have mentioned, since (according to its critics), it fails to allow for certain perfectly serious ethical concerns. It is thus, on this and other issues, a source of ethical insensitivity rather than of ethical insight.

As a doctrine, consequentialism owes its modern statement to Jeremy Bentham, the English radical and reformer of the late eighteenth and early nineteenth centuries, and in a particular and influential version, to John Stuart Mill, whose *Utilitarianism* was published in 1861.[3] (Given the dates of its modern founders, it might have been appropriate to consider this approach two chapters ago; but consequentialism's prominence in the shaping of public policy is an especially twentieth-century phenomenon, so it just as well appears on stage at this point in the story.) Consequentialism is the doctrine that actions are good and right solely in virtue of their consequences, and that action is right which maximizes good consequences. Utilitarianism is a version of consequentialism which identifies the maximization of utility, or happiness, as the particular consequence which matters most and should concern us – but there have been very many other versions, identifying different consequences, or

---

[3]   Jeremy Bentham's early and classic statement of his views is *An Introduction to the Principles of Morals and Legislation* of 1789.

outcomes, as specially significant. They have two things in common, which together form the basis of consequentialism's appeal.

First, consequentialism appeals to the fact that consequences really do matter to us in making moral judgments, and matter very much. The maxim "Let justice be done though the heavens fall" may have its exponents, but at the very least the potential fall of the heavens (assuming it to be a bad consequence) would properly cause us to pause before pressing on, however justly. Second, by making the production of happiness, for example, the common measure of all actions, consequentialism seems to offer the prospect of empirical commensurability in ethics, where previously there were conflicting, competing, and incommensurable principles and maxims. Suppose I am troubled by some conflict at work – I am duty bound to observe the company's whistle-blowing policy, but in so doing will have to reveal what was told to me in strictest confidence by a friend. Maybe – to make it even more difficult – blowing the whistle will not only breach the confidence, but will land that good friend in deep trouble, just when he is even now struggling to support a sick wife. Consequentialism promises to resolve my anxious sense of being bound by competing and seemingly irreconcilable claims by giving me a common currency (such as happiness), by which to assess and compare the fulfillment of these various duties. I now have only the one duty, and that is to do what will produce the best outcome. Suppose, on top of this resolution of competing obligations into one, the existence of a "felicific calculus" – a method for the calculation of happiness (such as some economists believe themselves possessed of); now difficult, troubling, and vexed ethical judgment may be replaced by an empirical science which delivers precise and clear decisions.

It is important, at this point, that the immediate appeal of consequentialism does not blind us to what is actually at stake. Consequences matter – it would be a very unusual account of ethics which overlooked or denied this claim. But consequentialism does not consist in the straightforward and uncontentious claim that consequences matter in the making of moral judgment, but rather in the doctrine that consequences are the *only* things that matter (and that if anything else matters, it is somehow because of its consequences). And this claim is far from being obviously true.

To see that its truth is far from obvious, take the matter of capital punishment. In a discussion we can well imagine the disputants trading claims as to whether or not capital punishment has a deterrent effect. Someone defends the practice because he or she believes that there is good evidence that it deters crime, whereas on the other side there are those who deny that there is such evidence, and for that very reason reject capital punishment. But this does not exhaust the sort of considerations which we might find deployed. We can very well imagine someone saying that they oppose capital punishment whether or not it deters; capital punishment, they say, is wrong in itself, no matter its consequences, just because it is wrong for the state to take life. One may or may not accept that argument, but that is not the immediate point; the immediate point is that the sort of thought we have mentioned is, in effect, dismissed out of hand by consequentialism, just because it is not a claim about consequences, whereas according to consequentialism, claims about consequences are not just important or even especially important in ethics, but exhaust ethics' proper concerns.

Now some concerns about biotechnology are indeed not only, or not even, claims about the consequences of our actions, but about the character of those actions. Suppose biotechnology puts into our hands the awesome powers over human nature which Jonas contemplates. Suppose, to take an example, biotechnology gives us the power to engineer better children – that is, children who are cleverer, taller, fitter, more beautiful, and possibly even more moral too. Certainly we might ask questions about the consequences of this policy, and such questions are likely to be very difficult to resolve and therefore somewhat vexed (in spite of consequentialism's promise to render ethical decisions easier). But even were we reassured about the consequences, might we not wonder whether there is something fundamentally wrong with the very project, in addition to any question of its consequences? Isn't this to instrumentalize our children? Shouldn't children first of all be accepted, rather than perfected – and doesn't the project we have envisaged enshrine a quite contrary view? Haven't children, in this scheme of things, been moved into the wrong category – just as if someone started to treat their friends as they treat their customers, or vice versa? Again, the point is not to say that these concerns are unquestionably compelling, but rather that they can't be dismissed out of hand when this is just what consequentialism does.

The problem we have identified, then, is that consequentialism seems to offer false reassurances; its failure to acknowledge certain worries indicates its lack of moral sensitivity, not the soundness of the state of affairs. But the consequentialist will, of course, reject any such thought, and insist instead on the validity of the fundamental claim that it really is consequences, and consequences alone, which matter. We should take seriously what consequentialism tells us about the nature and scope of ethics, its advocates will say, and put any other concerns to one side as so much muddle. So consequentialism has to be examined a bit more closely.

One aspect of consequentialism is captured in the maxim that "the ends justify the means" – that is, that good consequences may justify the doing of what otherwise appears wrong. The outcome is what counts and settles the moral reckoning one way or other. Now although utilitarianism and consequentialism are, as we have said, new terms, these positions systematize thoughts and notions which are much older – as is evidenced by the fact that Augustine wrote an attack on the contention that good ends may justify bad means right back at the end of the fourth century.

The occasion of his writing was as follows. Certain heretics, to escape detection, had taken to lying about their allegiances. The question then arose whether it would be licit for the orthodox to pretend allegiance to the heretical sect for the sake of catching them out. In other words, is it acceptable to lie and deceive for the sake of what is taken to be the very good end of detecting heretics?

The title of the treatise Augustine composed to address this issue, *Against Lying*, tells us the answer which he gave.[4] His reasons for providing this answer are many and varied. He points out that it is necessarily uncertain that the good consequences which a lie intends to bring about will be realized, whereas the lie and its wrongness are sure and certain. He also offers an argument from consequences against consequentialism – the thought is that it is all very well to consider what seems right in this one particular case, but the undermining of the institution or practice of truth-telling tends to a greater evil than the good which is here aimed at. (It is considerations of this kind which have very commonly led consequentialists, such as Mill, to defend a modified version of consequentialism, in his version sometimes called rule-utilitarianism. Rule-utilitarianism recognizes that moral rules may have a utility as rules of thumb, just because of the value of general practices of truth-telling, promise-keeping, returning of things loaned, and so on, which such rules instill and support. This move, however, for all its merit in seeming to defend consequentialism from an objection, is not without its problems: if observing the rule of thumb looks likely in a particular instance to result in poorer consequences than breaking the rule, why wouldn't the consequentialist break it? If they do break the rule, then what is left to the idea of "rule-utilitarianism" or "rule-consequentialism"? If they don't break it, what is left to the very idea of consequentialism?)

These, however, are not Augustine's main points, since he would be against lying even were the good results of lying certain, and the general tendency of such tactics not deleterious. His central point is rather that there are certain things which just ought not to be done: "thefts, fornications, [and] blasphemies" are on his list. The thought that evil may be done for the sake of good implies, however, that no action whatsoever, is, in principle, ruled out; but, as Augustine sees it, this is just a *reductio ad absurdum* of the position he is questioning. To translate

---

[4]   Augustine, *Against Lying*, trans. H. Browne, in *The Library of the Nicene and Post-Nicene Fathers*, 1st series, vol. 3 (repr. Edinburgh, 1988).

the point into modern terms, Augustine is claiming that there are certain actions (we might put torturing children, or discriminating on grounds of race or handicap, on our list) which are wrong and are known to be wrong more certainly than we know any metaethical claim – i.e. not ethical claims as such, but claims about such claims, here rules about rules and their justification. That is to say, to be specific: we know more certainly that it is wrong to torture children than we know the truth of any theory about ethics, such as that actions are good in virtue of their consequences. And since we know these primary moral truths very surely indeed, anything which discounts them (such as consequentialism), is a good target for attack by a *reductio ad absurdum*.

To see the force of this argument, consider an analogy. You propose a theory of what makes for a good drama. A good drama has to meet certain conditions as to plot, characterization, theme, language, and the like. On paper it seems plausible. But when we start to apply the theory of drama to plays we know, we find it gives us some startling results. Thus according to the theory Shakespeare's *Midsummer Night's Dream*, *Hamlet*, and *Romeo and Juliet* all turn out to be bad plays; so too, Racine's *Phèdre*, Chekov's *The Cherry Orchard*, and so on.

Now it would take a very strong faith in theory to stick to your guns and insist that these really are bad plays. More likely, the application of the theory will encourage us to wonder about its adequacy. We trust our first-order judgments about drama more than we trust our second-order reflections on a theory of drama – which is to say that our sense that *Hamlet* is a great play is likely (and properly) more secure than some theory we can devise about the nature of good drama.

So, to apply the analogy to moral judgments – the claim that we may do evil that good may come (that consequences are the only thing that matter), is a second-order theoretical judgment. And it comes into conflict with all sorts of first-order moral judgments: such as that one should not torture children, discriminate on grounds of sex or race, or whatever. Why would we abandon these moral judgments for the sake of a moral theory, which is what consequentialism is, just when this moral theory seems inherently less secure than these judgments?

This is not to say that the judgments to which we have appealed are immune from criticism and are simply fixed and immovable points; it is to say, however, that the relationship between theory and practical judgment in ethics is subtle, and in need of careful elaboration and consideration. But consequentialism is, of course, anything but subtle. Instead, it confronts many common and regular moral judgments with a bullying insistence on the rightness of its highly contentious claim that only consequences matter. Those who make the moral judgments we have indicated don't themselves need to reply with a countervailing dogmatism, such as that consequences don't matter one iota; it is enough for them to agree that consequences really do matter, and to say quietly, but firmly, that they are not the only thing that matter.

We mentioned that there are two regular problems with the discussion of biotechnology, these being bad science and bad ethics. Where there is bad science alarm bells ring when they should be silent; where there is poor ethics, the alarm bells stay quiet when they should be ringing. Now it is, as I have suggested, consequentialism which is very often responsible for the falsely reassuring silence of the alarms: there are questions which really matter which are simply not allowed by consequentialism. Amongst them would be the question about the application of biotechnology which we have already encountered, namely whether its invitation to treat nature, and even human nature, as raw material for our projects is the sort of invitation which we should be disinclined to accept at the outset.

Notice that so far, in trying to characterize the questions raised by biotechnology and its application, there has been no appeal to specifically Christian thoughts and ideas. Criticisms have been directed at mischaracterizations of the questions where such mischaracterizations arise from poor science and poor ethics; but in neither case did these criticisms rely on claims drawn from Christian doctrine or revelation. (It is true that Augustine would have noticed that the idea that one may do evil that good may come would place the Ten Commandments, for example, in some jeopardy; but there is no reason to read him as thinking that the wrongness of murder is something about which he would have been in doubt, were it not for its featuring on the list.) But this much said, we must return to the account of the situation which Jonas gave. According to Jonas, once we have understood the problem for itself and have seen the questions posed, we find ourselves at a loss in addressing them without appeal to religious reasons, just when these reasons are denied to us. We reach after the notion of the sacred, for example, which would stand in the way of our instrumentalizing nature, human or otherwise; but such notions have been repudiated by the science which has brought us to this point. If we want to go any further, in other words, it will be with religious ideas and notions which are essentially problematic.

It is interesting to notice that a number of weighty contemporary philosophers who have addressed questions concerned with nature and our respect for it have indeed found themselves turning to categories and concepts which lie somewhat outside our everyday discussions of right and wrong – such as "Promethean fear," "holy dread," "reverence," and "piety."[5] What is equally noteworthy, however, is that these same thinkers are clear in their own minds, at least, that they are not relying on theological resources in making their arguments. They have not, however, gone unchallenged.

A case in point is provided by Michael Sandel, Professor of Government at Harvard, and the author of *The Case against Perfection: Ethics in the Age of Genetic Engineering.*[6] His

[5] B. Williams, "Must a Concern for the Environment be Centred on Human Beings?", in *Making Sense of Humanity and Other Philosophical Papers* (Cambridge, 1995), 233–40; D. Wiggins, "Nature, Respect for Nature, and the Human Scale of Values," *Proceedings of the Aristotelian Society*, 100/1 (2000), 1–32; R. Scruton, *Animal Rights and Wrongs*, 3rd edn. (London, 2000), and "Epilogue: Notes Towards a Natural History of Religion," in M. Bentley, ed., *Public and Private Doctrine* (Cambridge, 1993), 251–69.

[6] Cambridge, MA, 2007. The book expands on a paper which first appeared as "The Case Against Perfection" in *The Atlantic Monthly* (Apr. 2004).

critique of genetic engineering rests on an appeal to the normative significance of what he terms the "gifted character" of human existence and attributes. In making this appeal, however, he has been suspected of smuggling religious concepts into his argument.[7]

As Sandel sees it, biotechnology allows and invites us to make and remake ourselves and others; just as Hans Jonas claimed, it seems to render "human nature" a project, rather than something to be accepted as a given. According to Sandel, "The problem with eugenics and genetic engineering is that they represent the one-sided triumph of willfulness over giftedness, of dominion over reverence, of molding over beholding."[8] But why should this triumph worry us? It would be founded, says Sandel, on a fundamental misconstrual of our relationships with one another, and in particular with our children. It would involve treating our children as something to be fixed and shaped, rather than as persons to be accepted and cherished.

Sandel's argument encounters a difficulty and an objection, however. Doesn't a gift need a giver? Or to put it another way, if we assert that there is an obligation to prefer "giftedness," "reverence," and "beholding" over "willfulness," "dominion," and "molding," isn't that because we are making surreptitious assumptions about the origins of nature, human or otherwise? Sandel's answers here are somewhat defensive. Religion, he says, is not the "only source of reasons to care about giftedness."[9] But he doesn't have a lot to say about these reasons and their alternative source. He thinks that there are other concepts which are associated with religious beliefs, without being dependent on them – the idea of the sanctity of life is one such.[10] But no sooner has he made the claim than, with commendable honesty, he points out a problem with it: "It might be replied that nontheological notions of sanctity and gift cannot ultimately

---

[7]   e.g. by Robert George and Carson Strong; see Sandel, *The Case Against Perfection*, 93 n. 5.
[8]   Sandel, *The Case Against Perfection*, 85.
[9]   *The Case Against Perfection*, 86.
[10]   *The Case Against Perfection*, 94.

stand on their own but must lean on borrowed metaphysical assumptions they fail to acknowledge." "This," says Sandel, "is a deep and difficult question that I cannot attempt to resolve here."[11]

The difficulty is, however, that this is precisely the question which has been put to him, and would surely be put to others who turn to the sort of notions and concepts which are commonly used to voice unease at the use of biotechnology. It is true enough that certain notions of "gift" and "giftedness" seem immediately unproblematic, just in the sense that they make no heavy metaphysical or religious assumptions whatsoever, even while they carry moral weight. Sandel notices such usage – if we describe someone's aptitude and talents as a gift, we mean to say just that these aptitudes and talents are not of their own making. And this claim alone is generally thought to have moral import – such as that we should, at the least, moderate our pride in these possessions, and that, having received them as a gift, we should be ready to use them with generosity. But this thought, which seems relatively uncontroversial, doesn't seem to amount to the sort of respect for "giftedness" which will do much work in constraining what we might or might not do with the tools of biotechnology in shaping or reshaping our given nature, or that of others.

Now at this point the contrast between Sandel's position and *certain* religious positions may come sharply into view – and this contrast perhaps explains the sense of rupture in relation to our moral framework to which Jonas points. What we might term pre-Kantian religion (i.e. that which holds to the metaphysical character of religious belief, which Kant ruled to be "beyond the bounds of reason alone") might insist, and insist strongly, that the world is a gift of God in the sense that such and such a birthday present was the gift of my father, something else a gift from my sister, and so on. God made the world and gave it to us (as my daughter made my birthday card and gave it to me), and this gift we need to respect. And arguably

11 Ibid.

respect for the gift may demand that we do not treat nature, human or otherwise, as just so much raw material to be molded and shaped to suit whatever ends we might have.

This is plainly not a position which Sandel would want to embrace; his sense of giftedness cannot be explicated or justified in this simple fashion. So the question returns: can we make alternative sense of this notion in such a way that it really might do some work, and yet not appeal to the sort of religious metaphysics to which Kant, Sandel's critics, and Sandel himself would object? The answer, I think, is that we can; and that in making sense of giftedness in this way, we can gain a better understanding of the role and place of post-Kantian religious belief in framing our moral world.

Whilst Kant in his critical philosophy banished claims about God from the realm of reason, he allowed that religious ideas and notions were, to use his terms, "necessary postulates of the practical reason"; that is, they were not themselves the grounds of obligations revealed to us by the practical reason, but rather could themselves be postulated on the basis of those obligations (though what there being "postulated" means precisely for Kant is a matter of some discussion). In developing a better sense of the place and role of religious ideas in contemporary discussion, we need to consider this approach a bit further, but we will certainly not want to argue that religious concepts and claims can be vindicated as implications of prior moral claims. It would be better to say neither that religion functions to ground the sense of giftedness (as pre-Kantian religion might suggest), nor that that sense of giftedness grounds religious concepts or belief (as a post-Kantian notion of "necessary postulates" might propose). Rather, we should say that religious notions and ideas are part of an imagining of the world and of our place in it, in which the sense of giftedness itself makes sense and carries weight. To this way of thinking, religious notions and concepts contribute to our framing of the world and human being, but are neither presuppositions nor implications of other claims.

To understand this point, we need to do two things. First, we need to notice that our moral lives make sense in the round, and are not a matter of a few principles which can be taken out of that wider context. Second, we need to notice how religious ideas and attitudes, as part of this moral life, may specifically provide a therapy of the desires – and how this may be a highly pertinent mode of engagement with the prospect afforded by biotechnology. It is this in which their weightiness consists, and in attributing such weight to religious notions, we don't need to go back to the sort of metaphysics at which Kant directed his strictures.

In expressing a concern or unease about biotechnology's relationship to nature (human and otherwise), there is understandably an inclination to turn to notions such as "givenness," as does Sandel. But Sandel rather reaches for this concept as if it were something which might be taken off a supermarket shelf. Moral concepts are, however, not like that. The concept of the "given" is, rather, part of a family of concepts. It is associated immediately with ideas of "respect" and "awe," and there finds itself rubbing shoulders with "reverence," "veneration," "worship," and even with ideas of "holiness" and "the sacred." Now these concepts and ideas and notions themselves have fields around them; and an account of how they function would not be immediately separable from a description of these fields, nor, just as importantly, from the further ideas of nature and human nature to which they may be related. There is here a very complex "moral ecology" as we might term it – that is, our understanding and experience of the world are fixed by the complexity of our descriptions and evaluations, which are not themselves readily separable. Certainly there are no lines of inference which can be traced going in one or other direction, from description to evaluation, or from evaluation to description. And certainly we cannot simply remove one concept from this network, and subject it to an examination which dissociates it from the network of relationships in which its place and significance are fixed – which is to say that the notion of "gift" and "giftedness" cannot be treated as Sandel and his critics are inclined to treat it. It needs instead to be located in an anthropology of morality – a rich description of the form of life in which this and related concepts and ideas have their place, purpose, and significance.

   This is a major task. It would involve a detailed mapping of the ways in which we speak, think, and act in relation to nature and the natural world – since this is the context from which, and in which, talk about "gifts" and "giftedness" makes sense. Returning to the debate with an understanding of this moral world, it would readily make sense, I suspect, not only to insist that gifts do not need givers (a point which is true of our talents, for example), but moreover that to speak of certain things as gifts is just to characterize them as the sort of things which are to be accepted and cherished for what they are, rather than treated as ours to do with as we will. This is not true of all gifts of course. When a great-aunt gives me a sweater which certainly would have seemed tasteful to my great-uncle thirty years ago, I doubtless have certain obligations in regard to it – even though it is a gift, I can't simply do with it as I will. Putting it on the fire immediately, for example, would be unacceptable. But it might be compatible with respecting this gift that I quietly dispose of it to a charity shop the Christmas following the one on which I received it. Not so with the children we describe as "gifts," nor arguably with nature or human nature. To speak of these as gifts is just to say that they are properly received only as they are accepted for what they are, and welcomed as such. They cannot be repudiated. Or at least, if they are, we simply haven't understood what it meant to call them "gifts."
   Sandel's critics are wrong, then, to accuse him of needing a concept of giftedness which is dependent on high metaphysics. On the contrary, if what I have suggested is true, this and other such concepts may function neither as implications of such a metaphysics, nor even as "postulates of the practical reason" in Kant's (somewhat uncertain) sense. Instead, we can see that this and related concepts are part of a complex web of ways in which we speak, think, and act, through which we understand and value the world. And we might well suggest that our practices, properly described, become perfectly intelligible to the actors and to sensitive observers, without any further assumptions or argument. That we recognize moral obligations, including the subtle and complex obligations defined by the language of gift, reverence, respect, and so on, is a fact about us, just as

that we have friends, or play music or games. None of these needs a justification.

Now just as we can see that we need no high metaphysics, religious or otherwise, to warrant concerns about biotechnology, so we can see too, I think, that the weightiness of these concerns, and their power, is not only a matter of their being used in an argument in any very obvious sense. It is rather that they can play a role in the therapy of desires which is central to religion's contribution to the ethical life, just as St. Benedict presupposed in founding a school aimed not at increasing knowledge, but at disciplining the will.

To be relevant to the problem of biotechnology, it is not the case that religion must furnish us with distinctive beliefs about the world and its origins, nor even with specific and unique moral injunctions. It might also be relevant as it provides a therapy for our sometimes disordered relationship to the world, simply perhaps by reminding us that there is another and better way of being in the world. And this contribution can be profoundly important.

It is, of course, the natural error of a philosopher to suppose that what is needed is argument, and that where an argument doesn't seem to be working, what is needed is more and better argument and the burnishing of reasons. But this may very well not be what is needed. The argument may not be at fault. The reasons may be perfectly good reasons as far as we can tell. It is just that in spite of the worthiness of the reasons, they don't get a purchase on the case in hand.

Consider the following perfectly familiar instance. There is no harm in a concern for one's material well-being most of the time, but it is doubtless true that most of the time, most of us are mostly too concerned with it. This is probably, though it sounds rather odd, both selfish and not selfish enough (as Butler would have said). Selfish, because there are others whose well-being we ought to be concerned with, and not selfish enough because being concerned with those others would (nearly every survey seems to suggest) make us happier. Either way, when we reason like this (or are reasoned with) we may very well change our thoughts, plans, inclinations, and, most importantly of all, our actions. Not so, however, in every case. There are those who are impervious to reasoning of this kind. Amongst them, and at the extreme, there are those we call misers, in whom the everyday and harmless, and indeed perhaps essential, interest in material security has become so dominant as to be wholly perverse. But, of course, in this case, we are not inclined to think that polishing our denunciations of meanness would do the trick. The "should not" just doesn't get a purchase, even if the reasons are perfectly good ones.

We might say something similar about someone who is fascinated and obsessed with pornography. We can very probably give a convincing account of what is wrong here. The person who has settled into a comfortable relationship with pornography, perhaps out of loneliness, is very possibly damaging their chances of ever addressing that loneliness in a far more effective and appropriate manner. In the absence of genuine relationships (involving mutuality, spontaneity, and emotional depth), he (one doesn't in this case need the otherwise obligatory "or she") has turned to fantastic caricatures of such relationships – in which, of course, there is unchallenged power, reliable routine, and convenient superficiality. All this may be true. But we also know, without doubting the force of the arguments, that it would be quite hopeless for a counselor to try wean a client from his dependence on pornography by describing the characteristics of a genuine relationship (namely mutuality, spontaneity, and emotional depth), when it is the immediate attraction of the opposites (power, routine, and superficiality) which explains the dependence. The fact that the counselor's argument wouldn't serve doesn't indicate, however, that it is not good as an argument, even as it stands – it is simply that it is eclipsed in this case, and needs some other sort of assistance than the assistance which might come from finding even better reasons. It is reason which has failed; it is not reason, as such, which is the solution.

In an aside, Wittgenstein once remarked: "If you find yourself stumped trying to convince someone of something and not getting anywhere, tell yourself that it is the *will* and not the intellect that you're up against."[12] Of course, as a general presupposition this would seem to license the very dangerous assumption that the failure of an opponent to acknowledge the power of one's reasoning is always willful. But Wittgenstein did not mean that – he meant to say that sometimes we want to cling to certain theories for deeper reasons than we may admit or even ourselves understand. And then what is needed is what Wittgenstein himself referred to as "therapy" – meaning, by analogy with the practice of Freudian analysis, the patient attempt to discern the hidden reasons which constrain our thoughts and actions, even against other reasons and thoughts we may have.

The miser needs therapy, not argument. He or she does not need new information about the benefits or otherwise of hoarding one's money. The miser has not, so to say, made a miscalculation, which can be corrected by fresh information. What is needed is a new vantage point and one which is likely to be already available to the miser if only he or she could be brought to attend to it. Thus it is with George Eliot's great miser, Silas Marner: it is a golden-haired foundling who teaches him how properly to value gold of a different kind and who is thus the cause of the dawning of a new life. A brush with death might have had the same effect; or it might be overhearing some account of how others regard us and realizing, with a sense of horror, that this really is how we appear to others; maybe it is a story which moves us to reorder our lives; or it could even be that a single joke provides us with a new and liberating perspective on a situation. These may each be therapeutic simply by helping us to reckon with what we actually know already in a certain way, but, for whatever reason, fail to live by. Therapy then, addresses the reason, but the reason of the heart.

Now what has this to do with nature, biotechnology, reason, and religion, which is where this chapter began? Jonas found the "novum" of biotechnology not just in the power over nature and human nature which it puts into our hands, but also the

---

[12]   Cited by P. M. S. Hacker, in *Wittgenstein's Place in Twentieth Century Philosophy* (Oxford, 1996), 113.

impetus which attaches to its use. Technology has become, he says, humankind's "most significant enterprise, in whose permanent, self-transcending advance to ever greater things the vocation of man tends to be seen, and whose success of maximal control over things and himself appears as the consummation of his destiny.... [With technology] [o]utshining in prestige and starving in resources whatever else belongs to the fullness of man, the expansion of his power is accompanied by a contraction of his self-conception and being."[13]

If this was true in 1974, it seems no less true some thirty-five years later. The discourse around the Human Genome Project echoed the discourse surrounding the moon landings of the 1960s; the talk was of discovery and destiny, imbuing the expenditure of some $3 billion with an aura of inevitability. The obligation is to a bright new future, in which the understanding of our genetic constitutions promises better prevention, diagnosis, and treatment of disease – indeed, in which it promises the virtual eradication of disease. And the obligation to this future takes on the character of a moral imperative – as in talk of "the war against cancer," there is an enemy which we must defeat, almost as if our survival depends on it.

It is difficult to say whether this presentation of the future itself shapes our understanding of the present, or depends upon it. Whichever it is, it is certainly the case that this vision of the future goes along with a somewhat anxious account of the human present. For the obligingness of this future seems to suppose the deep unsatisfactoriness of the here and now. And the sense of the unsatisfactory nature of the present seems much in evidence. Strangely, at a time when life expectancies in the affluent West are at levels which would have astonished our grandparents, let alone our great-grandparents, we have become anxious consumers of stories which treat our health as a subject of intense interest and concern – stories on the latest treatment for this and that, coverage of great new discoveries which promise to banish this or that complaint, sensational claims for the virtues of eating beetroot or the perils of eating too much meat.

[13]   Jonas, "Technology and Responsibility," 11.

It is as if we think our lives especially fragile just as they have never been more secure; as if we found people who lived in a land of plenty, endlessly worried about the risks of famine. Life has to be corrected, saved, extended, perfected, improved, shaped, modified, and enhanced. It is as if the present falls short and is a disappointment to us; or worse, it is a place of fear and frustration which is bearable only as we place our hope in the promise of something better (which, ironically, is the dubious role which some, such as Marx, have attributed to religion).

What are we to make of this? We live in a time of unprecedented good health and – previously undreamt of – life expectancy and yet also in a time of considerable anxiety about health and life expectancy. We live in a time in which the bold, bright future promised by medical technologies summons us with all the force of a categorical imperative; so much so that we in the West invest larger and larger amounts in medical research which promises benefits at the margins, when tiny amounts spent elsewhere in the world would bring huge and manifest gains for those who lack basic health care and even the very necessities of life. We behave as if we are living in a deeply unsatisfactory present, and invest our hopes in a future which will allow us to reach our proper potential and fullness. We might be tempted to observe of ourselves what De Tocqueville said of the inhabitants of the United States, some two hundred years ago: "In America I have seen the freest and best educated of men in circumstances the happiest to be found in the world, yet it seemed to me that a cloud habitually hung on their brow, and they seemed serious and almost sad even in their pleasures."[14]

In an article written in the mid 1960s and entitled "The Problem of Genetic Manipulation," the Jesuit theologian Karl Rahner asserts, rather baldly, that "Genetic manipulation is the embodiment of the fear of oneself, the fear of accepting one's self as the unknown quantity it is." He went on to suggest that the driving forces behind genetic manipulation were hate, fear,

---

[14]   A. de Tocqueville, *Democracy in America*, in many editions; Book 2, pt. 2, ch. 12.

and despair at one's destiny.[15] Such a thesis might need softening in a number of ways, but at least it has the merit of giving us some explanation of what would otherwise seem quite mysterious, namely the sense of urgency and obligation which is attached to the task of ameliorating the human lot through biotechnology, notwithstanding that we live "in circumstances the happiest to be found."

The imperative to biotechnology, like the imperative which drives the miser, seems disproportionate. As the miser invests in money an interest and importance it cannot ultimately bear, so it may be that we have come to invest in technology, medical and otherwise, an urgency and interest which is equally fantastic. The pathos of Sandel's argument, in the end, is then not that he give reasons of insufficient strength, but that the giving of reasons somehow misses the point. A society which has invested so much, emotionally and materially and imaginatively, in the project of mastering nature of which modern-day genomic science is the most dizzying example, will not hear a forbidding of such strategies. In place of a stronger "must not" or "should not" it needs to hear a more powerful and liberating "need not." And, to adopt a theological way of putting it, we shouldn't be simply Pelagian here – which is to say that the giving of reasons will probably not be sufficient to give us pause, when it is our hearts, like the hearts of the miser, which need to be kindled afresh.

Religion speaks to the heart. It can offer a therapy of our desires. We began with Benedict, and, even in an age of genetic engineering, we can end with Benedict. In his day, and in ours, the practice of the Christian life centers around the stories contained in the Scriptures. These stories, with or without metaphysics, have the power to inspire humility, worship, and service. They will give us new thoughts and inclinations in regard to forgiveness, justice, and charity. And to the extent that we live by these stories we may discover a way of being in the world and with one another which is distinctive and critical – not just in history, but in the present.

[15]   K. Rahner, "The Problem of Genetic Manipulation," in *Theological Investigations*, vol. 9 (New York, 1973).

Suggestions for Further Reading

An obvious way for readers to take further their exploration of Christian ethics is to turn to the authors and leading texts which have been mentioned or discussed in the preceding chapters. Of course the Bible is the text which, in various ways, has concerned, formed, and constrained the work of every Christian thinker. A way into the most important of the biblical material for the Christian tradition, and an introduction to the issues posed by its interpretation, is provided with great sophistication and insight by Richard Hays in *The Moral Vision of the New Testament*.

Augustine's reading of the Bible and understanding of Christianity have been fundamental to the subsequent Western tradition (and this book has not attempted to deal with the Eastern Orthodox tradition). Augustine's *Confessions* was extremely influential in the Middle Ages, but *The City of God* gives a better sense of the grounding of his ethical concerns in the broad sweep of his theological framework. Book 14, his attempt to understand the created order as good yet fallen, is crucial; Book 22 treats of the resurrection, and shows how thoroughly affirming of the goodness of the body he was. His *Letters* provide the best insight into his approach to matters of immediate practical significance, especially in relation to the problem of capital punishment (an interesting selection is found in the collection of *Political Writings* referred to in the Bibliography). Peter Brown's *Augustine of Hippo* is a compelling and authoritative account of the development of Augustine's thought against the background of his historical context and life. (This course of reading would give the lie, by the way, to the popular prejudice that Augustine was obsessed with matters to do with sex.)

It would be a pity to read the other so-called patristic writers only to heighten one's sense of the incomparable scope and complexity of Augustine's contribution, but that may indeed be a side effect of so doing. The first 400 years of the Christian era provide many works of interest: Clement of Alexandria's sermon "Who is the rich man that shall be saved?" is, for example, an important contribution to the early Fathers' common concern for questions of wealth and poverty; and Tertullian wrote short and sharp treatises on many obviously ethical issues. But it is worth stressing that "ethics" is not approached as a separate subject, so that, as with Augustine, a real understanding of how early Christians thought about the world and their life within it can only be gleaned from attention to wider theological concerns and writings. Peter Brown's *The Body and Society* takes this point very seriously, and is an insightful and fully referenced guide to four centuries of controversy over questions to do with virginity, celibacy, and marriage.

On the far side of the gulf between the *Rule of St Benedict* from the sixth century, and where we next picked up the story, stands Aquinas's *Summa Theologiae*, a work which is difficult to approach because of its sheer bulk (60 volumes in the English translation), and its dense construction as a textbook, contrasting and resolving the views of different authorities. The beginner can be further deterred by solemn warnings that each part must be seen in the context of the whole; this is doubtless true, but it seems probable that anyone inclined to take this warning seriously is more likely to refrain altogether from reading the work, than be inspired to begin at the beginning and read to the end. The best thing to do is to scan the list of subjects in the various parts of the *Summa* and start reading wherever your interest directs you – remaining aware, however, of the need to test any initial judgments on what Aquinas does or doesn't think by reference to even wider reading.

Martin Luther is well served by his modern biographers, and Marius's *Martin Luther*, for example, provides the necessary context in which to see *The Freedom of a Christian*. Luther's contributions to particular controversies and concerns of obvious ethical import are helpfully gathered in volumes 44–7 of the American edition of Luther's works, and again the reader may follow any particular interest. Luther's address *Against the Robbing and Murdering Hordes of Peasants* of 1525 (in volume 46), has had a certain notoriety from the day it was first written, and might be read to encourage the posing of questions about the meaning and significance of Luther's repudiation of casuistry. Whether Luther's near contemporary Michel de Montaigne is judged to be a contributor to Christian thought or rather a critic of it, is something of a moot point; but within his *Essays*, his essay on "Cannibalism" is indicative of his concerns and approach (and charm).

Amongst the eighteenth- and early nineteenth-century figures who address the moral skepticism which is sometimes blamed on Luther and associated with Montaigne, Butler has the merit of doing so very briefly. His "Dissertation on the Nature of Virtue" provides a short and lucid statement in defense of the authority of morals. Kant's moves on behalf of the "moral law" are neither short nor lucid. By all means the reader should attempt *The Groundwork of the Metaphysics of Morals*, but with the very same spirit as one would attempt the ascent of Everest; don't be surprised, in other words, if it is difficult and one is left gasping for breath. (*The Cambridge Companion to Kant*, edited by P. Guyer, has an introduction which helpfully surveys Kant's wider concerns and achievement.) Kierkegaard's protest on behalf of "authentic Christianity" in *Fear and Trembling* is relatively short amongst his works, but by no means easy. In order to place it in the context of Kierkegaard's vast and complex corpus, guidance should be sought from Hannay's intellectual biography, *Kierkegaard*.

Nietzsche wanted no interpreter but himself; however that may be, Scheler's *Ressentiment* is undoubtedly helpful in highlighting something of the importance (and limits) of *The Genealogy of Morals*. Mill's *Utilitarianism* is somewhat more approachable; equally approachable is the last chapter of Williams's little book *Morality*, with its brief and telling indication of some of the problems with consequentialism.

John Paul II's *Veritatis Splendor* touches on this issue, and on the issue of moral relativism. Along with *Evangelium Vitae*, it provides a clear and reasoned introduction to the various challenges facing ethical, and more specifically Christian ethical, thought at the end of the twentieth century. Barth's great work, *Church Dogmatics*, is not intended as a work of apologetics in the same way, but the power of his exposition of the meaning of doctrine for human action is immense; his treatment of "Man and Woman" in volume III/4 provides a way into the larger work. The unfinished fragment, *The Christian Life*, the beginning of an exposition of the Lord's Prayer, is equally rich and impressive. Busch's biography of Barth can be recommended to those who, unaware of the historical context in which Barth and Bonhoeffer contended, are prone to find them both somewhat too insistent.

The focus of the last chapter of this book on one particular topic, bioethics, was meant to indicate that the tradition of thought and debate which has been the subject of the previous chapters can and should be brought to contemporary concerns. For those who wish to explore this engagement further, Lammers and Verhey's *On Moral Medicine* is a book of readings from a huge variety of sources addressing one very broad theme of controversy. My own *Christian Ethics and Contemporary Moral Problems* is an attempt to venture into that and other areas, and touches on questions to do with the beginning and end of life, the environment, the use of animals in biotechnology, and sexual ethics.

Bibliography

Primary Sources

Particular editions are not given where a book is widely available and no specific version has been relied on in the text.

Aquinas. *Aquinas: Selected Political Writings*, ed. A. P. D'Entrèves, trans. J. G. Dawson (Oxford, 1959).

Aquinas. *Summa Theologiae*, 1a2ae, 90–7; vol. 28 of the Blackfriars edition, trans. T. Gilby (London, 1966).

Aristotle. *The Eudemian Ethics*, trans. H. Rackham (London, 1952).

Augustine. *Against Lying*, trans. H. Browne, in *The Library of the Nicene and Post-Nicene Fathers*, 1st series, vol. 3 (repr. Edinburgh, 1988).

Augustine. *The City of God*, trans. H. Bettenson (Harmondsworth, 1984).

Augustine. *Confessions*, trans. H. Chadwick (Oxford, 1991).

Augustine. *Contra Julianum*, trans. M. A. Schumacher (Washington, 1957).

Augustine. *On Marriage and Concupiscence*, trans. P. Holmes and R. Wallis, *Nicene and Post-Nicene Fathers*, 1st series, vol. 5 (Edinburgh, 1991).

Augustine. *Political Writings*, ed. E. M. Atkins and R. J. Dodaro, trans. E. M. Atkins (Cambridge, 2001).

Barth, K. *The Christian Life*, trans. G. W. Bromiley (Edinburgh, 1981).

Barth, K. *Church Dogmatics*, I. 2, trans. G. Thomson and H. Knight (Edinburgh, 1956); III. 2, trans. H. Knight et al. (Edinburgh, 1960); and III. 4, trans. A. Mackay et al. (Edinburgh, 1961).

Benedict. *The Rule of St Benedict*, trans. J. McCann (London, 1976).

Bentham, J. *An Introduction to the Principles of Morals and Legislation* (first published 1789).
Bonhoeffer, D. *Discipleship*, trans. B. Green and R. Krauss (Minneapolis, 2001).
Butler, J. "A Dissertation Upon the Nature of Virtue" (first published as an appendix to Book 1, ch. 3, of Butler's *Analogy of Religion* of 1736).
Clement of Alexandria. "Who is the rich man that shall be saved?," trans. W. Wilson, *Ante-Nicene Fathers*, vol. 2 (Edinburgh, 1994).
Darwin, C. *The Descent of Man* (London, 1871).
Hobbes, T. *Leviathan* (first published 1651).
Hume, D. *An Enquiry Concerning the Principles of Morals*, in *Enquiries*, ed. L. A. Selby-Bigge, 3rd edn. (Oxford, 1975).
Jerome. *Letters*, trans. W. H. Freemantle, *Nicene and Post-Nicene Fathers*, 2nd series, vol. 6, repr. (Edinburgh, 1989).
John Paul II. *Evangelium Vitae* (London, 1995).
John Paul II. *Veritatis Splendor* (London, 1993).
Kant, I. *Conflict of the Faculties*, trans. M. Gregor, in *Religion and Rational Theology: The Cambridge Edition of the Works of Immanuel Kant* (Cambridge, 1996).
Kant, I. *Critique of Practical Reason*, trans. and ed. M. Gregor (Cambridge, 1997).
Kant, I. *Groundwork of the Metaphysic of Morals*, trans. H. J. Paton as *The Moral Law* (London, 1948).
Kierkegaard, S. *Fear and Trembling*, trans. H. V. Hong and E. H. Hong (Princeton, 1983).
Luther, M. *Against the Robbing and Murdering Hordes of Peasants*, trans. C. M. Jacobs, in *Luther's Works*, vol. 46 (Philadelphia, 1967).
Luther, M. *The Disputation Against Scholastic Theology*, trans. H. J. Grimm, in *Luther's Works*, vol. 31 (Philadelphia, 1957).
Luther, M. *The Freedom of a Christian*, trans. W. A. Lambert, in *Luther's Works*, vol. 31 (Philadelphia, 1957).
Luther, M. *On Secular Authority*, in *Luther and Calvin on Secular Authority*, ed. and trans. H. Höpfl (Cambridge, 1991).
Luther, M. *Ten Sermons on the Catechism*, trans. in *Luther's Works*, vol. 51 (Philadelphia, 1959).
Marx, K. *The Communist Manifesto* (first published 1848).
Mill, J. S. *Utilitarianism* (first published 1861).
Montaigne, M. de. *An Apology for Raymond Sebond*, trans. M. A. Screech (London, 1987).

Montaigne, M. de. *Essays*, trans. E. J. Trechmann (London, 1935).
Nietzsche, F. *Human, All Too Human*, trans. R. J. Hollingdale (Cambridge, 1986).
Nietzsche, F. *On the Genealogy of Morals*, trans. C. Diethe (Cambridge, 1994).
Nietzsche, F. *Thus Spoke Zarathustra*, trans. A. del Caro (Cambridge, 2006).
Plato. *The Republic*.
Tocqueville, A. de. *Democracy in America*, 2 vols. (1835 and 1840).
Vitoria, F. de. *Political Writings*, ed. and trans. A. Pagden and J. Lawrance (Cambridge, 1991).

Secondary Sources

Atwood, M. *Oryx and Crake* (London, 2003).
Banner, M. *Christian Ethics and Contemporary Moral Problems* (Cambridge, 1999).
Brown, P. *Augustine of Hippo* (London, 1967).
Brown, P. *The Body and Society: Men, Women and Sexual Renunciation in Early Christianity* (London, 1989).
Bulger, R. E., E. Heitman, and S. J. Reiser, eds., *The Ethical Dimensions of the Biological Sciences* (Cambridge, 1993).
Busch, E. *Karl Barth* (London, 1976).
Catechism of the Catholic Church, English trans. (London, 1994).
Copleston, F. C. *Aquinas* (Harmondsworth, 1955).
Ebeling, G. *Luther: An Introduction to his Thought*, trans. R. A. Wilson (London, 1970).
Fodor, J. "Reading the Scriptures: Rehearsing Identity, Practicing Character," in S. Hauerwas and S. Wells, *The Blackwell Companion to Christian Ethics* (Oxford, 2004), 141–55.
Garnsey, P. *Ideas of Slavery from Aristotle to Augustine* (Cambridge, 1996).
Guyer, P. ed. *The Cambridge Companion to Kant* (Cambridge, 1992).
Hacker, P. M. S. *Wittgenstein's Place in Twentieth Century Philosophy* (Oxford, 1996).
Hannay, A. *Kierkegaard: A Biography* (Cambridge, 2001).
Hauerwas, S. *The Peaceable Kingdom* (London, 1984).
Hays, R. *The Moral Vision of the New Testament* (London, 1997).
Hittenger, R. "Natural Law and Catholic Moral Theology," in M. Cromartie, ed., *A Preserving Grace* (Washington, 1997), 1–30.

Jonas, H. "Technology and Responsibility: Reflections on the New Tasks of Ethics," in *Philosophical Essays* (Chicago, 1974), 3–20.

Lancel, S. *St Augustine*, trans. A. Nevill (London, 2002).

Lammers, S., and A. Verhey, eds. *On Moral Medicine* 2nd edn. (Grand Rapids, 1998).

MacIntyre, A. *After Virtue* (London, 1981).

Marius, R. *Martin Luther: The Christian Between Life and Death* (London, 1999).

Pinkaers, S. *Sources of Christian Ethics*, trans. M. T. Noble (Edinburgh, 1995).

Putnam, R. H. *Bowling Alone: The Collapse and Revival of American Community*, new edn. (New York, 2000).

Rachels, J. *Created from Animals* (London, 1990).

Rahner, K. "The Problem of Genetic Manipulation," in *Theological Investigations*, vol. 9 (New York, 1973), 205–22.

Sandel, M. *The Case Against Perfection: Ethics in the Age of Genetic Engineering* (Cambridge, MA, 2007).

Scheler, M. *Ressentiment*, trans. L. B. Coser and W. W. Holdheim (Milwaukee, 1998).

Scruton, R. *Animal Rights and Wrongs*, 3rd edn. (London, 2000).

Scruton, R. "Epilogue: Notes Towards a Natural History of Religion," in M. Bentley, ed., *Public and Private Doctrine* (Cambridge, 1993), 251–69.

Walzer, M. *Thick and Thin: Moral Arguments at Home and Abroad* (Notre Dame, 1994).

Wannenwetsch, B. "Luther's Moral Theology," in D. K. McKim, ed., *The Cambridge Companion to Martin Luther* (Cambridge, 2003), 120–35.

Watson, P. S. *Let God be God! An Interpretation of the Theology of Martin Luther* (London, 1947).

Wiggins, D. "Nature, Respect for Nature, and the Human Scale of Values," *Proceedings of the Aristotelian Society*, 100/1 (2000), 1–32.

Williams, B. *Morality: An Introduction to Ethics* (Cambridge, 1976).

Williams, B. "Must a Concern for the Environment be Centred on Human Beings?," in *Making Sense of Humanity and Other Philosophical Papers* (Cambridge, 1995), 233–40.

Index

BJ
1201
.B36
2009